The Debate on Higher Education

Challenging the Assumptions

Adrian Seville
City University, London

and

James Tooley
University of Manchester

Published by the IEA Education and Training Unit, 1997

First published in October 1997 by
The Institute of Economic Affairs
2 Lord North Street
Westminster
London SW1P 3LB

© IEA 1997

IEA Studies in Education No. 5
All rights reserved

ISBN 0-255 36409-1

Many IEA publications are translated into languages other than English or are reprinted. Permission to translate or to reprint should be sought from the General Director at the address above.

Printed in Great Britain by
Hartington Fine Arts Limited, Lancing, West Sussex
Set in Century Schoolbook and Bookman Old Style

Contents

Foreword *Professor Colin Robinson*	7
The Authors	8
Acknowledgements	9

Higher Education Without the State

A Critical Introduction to Adrian Seville's The Radical Implications of Modularity

James Tooley

1	**Seville's Contribution**	13
	What is Higher Education?	16
	Government Intervention in Higher Education	16
	Format of the Paper	17
2	**Justifications for State Intervention in Higher Education**	18
	Without the State, no Higher Education Opportunities?	18
	The 'Advancement of Learning' as a Charitable Activity	18
	Without the State, *Particular* Sorts of Higher Education not Provided?	20
	War and the Expansion of Higher Education Control	22
	Robbins' Hidden Agenda	23
	Externalities of Higher Education	28
	Negative Externalities of Government Intervention in Higher Education	29
	No Need for State Intervention in Higher Education	32

3	**Equity and Social Justice**	34
	Equity and Entrance Requirements	34
	Inequity in State Intervention in Higher Education	36
	Income-Contingent Loans for Greater Access to Higher Education	36
	Robbins and Income-Contingent Loans	38
	Privatised Income-Contingent Loans	40
	The Information Problem	41
4	**The Future of Higher Education: HE without the State**	43
	References/Bibliography	46

The Radical Implications of Modularity

Adrian Seville

1	**Introduction**	51
2	**Modular and Traditional Schemes**	55
	Characteristics of Traditional Higher Education: the Cohort Scheme	55
	Characteristics of Higher Education in the Modular Scheme	56
	Provision of Modular Higher Education	58
	Organisation of the Modular Scheme	59
	Semesterisation	60
	Pressures for Modularisation: Diversity of Student Intake	60
	Strengths and Weaknesses of the Modular Scheme	62

	Distortions of the Market in Higher Education	65
3	**Quality**	**68**
	Quality Control in Higher Education	68
	Relativism in Standards	70
	What is a Degree?	71
	Measurement of Success	74
	The 'Learning Outcomes' Debate	76
	Disturbing Conclusions on Quality	78
	Developments by the Funding Councils and HEQC	79
	Alternative Policy in the Context of Modular Education	80
	Explicit Categorisation of Objectives	81
4	**Funding**	**84**
	Present Funding and the Student Experience	84
	Addressing the Funding Gap in Undergraduate Courses	86
	Alternative Funding Mechanisms	90
	Problems in Funding of Alternative Modes of Study	90
	Robertson's Over-arching Proposals	92
	Unsuitability of Credit-Based Funding	93
	Provision-based Funding	94
	Dangers of Output-related Funding and 'Value Added' Measures	100
	The HEFCE Consultation on the Funding Method for Teaching	101
5	**Evolution of Institutions in the Higher Education System**	**103**

Appendix A: UGC and UFC Funding Systems for Higher Education	108
Funding Models	108
The Instability of the UFC Funding Model of 1991	110
Assumption of the Projection	110
Methodology	110
Discussion of the Projections	111
Appendix B: Analysis of HEFC University Funding	116
Average Units of HEFCE Funding	116
Comparison of Teacher Funding	116
Figures	
1. The Cohort Scheme	57
2. The Modular Scheme	57
3. UFC Funded Student Numbers	113
4. Student Numbers – Total Funded and Unfunded	114
5. Unit of Resource	115
6. Teacher Funding 1993-94	118
References/Bibliography	119
Summary	*Back Cover*

Foreword

Publication of *The Debate on Higher Education* marks a timely challenge, post-Dearing, to the assumptions on which British higher education has for many years been founded.

Dr Adrian Seville, Academic Registrar of City University, London, points out the radical implications of the move towards 'modularity' in universities and shows how this move is capable of introducing market-like mechanisms. In doing so, he raises fundamental questions about the nature of a degree, the effects of the way universities are funded and the adequacy of quality controls. Dr James Tooley, Director of the Institute's Education and Training Unit, complements Adrian Seville's paper by stepping back from existing controversies, going back to first principles and investigating to what extent government involvement in higher education can be justified. He analyses in some depth the arguments commonly used in support of such involvement and finds them wanting.

By bringing into the open issues which are rarely made explicit, Drs Tooley and Seville significantly raise the level of the debate about higher education. The Institute publishes their paper as an important contribution to that debate although, as in all IEA papers, the views are those of the authors not of the Institute (which has no corporate view), its Trustees, Advisers or Directors.

October 1997 COLIN ROBINSON
Editorial Director, Institute of Economic Affairs;
Professor of Economics, University of Surrey

The Authors

Adrian Seville is the Academic Registrar of City University, London. He was an Open Scholar of Trinity Hall, Cambridge, where he read Natural Sciences. He obtained his PhD in the physics of metals from Edinburgh University, where he joined the academic staff. Subsequently, he moved to City University, first as Lecturer in Physics, then Senior Lecturer. He became Deputy Academic Registrar in 1977, being appointed to his present post in 1982. He has been interested in issues of credit accumulation and transfer in Higher Education for many years. He was active on the relevant committees of the CNAA and, more recently, has contributed to the HEQC CAT Development Project, with special reference to the funding aspects of the university system. At City University, he is – among other things – responsible for strategic academic planning and defining the University's position in the market.

James Tooley is University Research Fellow at the School of Education, University of Manchester, and is Director of the Education and Training Unit at the Institute of Economic Affairs. His PhD, in philosophy of education, is from the Institute of Education, University of London. Previously, he held research posts at the University of Oxford's Department of Educational Studies and the National Foundation for Educational Research. He also taught courses in philosophy and sociology of education at Homerton College, University of Cambridge; University of East London; University of the Western Cape, South Africa; and Simon Fraser University, Canada. He serves on the Executive Committee of the Philosophy of Education Society of Great Britain. Before entering educational research, he was a mathematics teacher in Zimbabwe and London.

Acknowledgements

Among several friends and colleagues who have commented on this paper in draft form, particular mention is to be made of Professor Geoffrey Wood, of the Department of Banking and Finance at City University, whose encouragement and advice have been invaluable.

A. S.

Professor David Conway of Middlesex University invited me to give a paper on higher education and the state which prompted this paper. I am grateful to him and to participants at his seminar for helpful comments and challenges. As always, thanks to Professor Colin Robinson for his friendly and generous support.

J. T.

Higher Education Without the State?

A Critical Introduction to Adrian Seville's *The Radical Implications of Modularity*

James Tooley, University of Manchester

1 | Seville's Contribution

With the publication of the National Committee of Inquiry's report (the 'Dearing Report'), higher education in the UK is at a crucial juncture in its history. Its funding is in crisis, and morale amongst academics is perilously low, in part brought down by the burden of bureaucratic, government-imposed quality control procedures. Students, too, feel they are getting a raw deal, bemused that previously-accepted levels of living grants and free tuition are under threat, that traditional standards of scholarly attention are eroded, while at the same time, rampant qualification inflation undermines their paper achievements. Many in the universities and outside wonder, too, whether quality can be maintained in the bewildering expansion of institutions brought by government fiat under the rubric of 'university'. All these factors, of course, inspired the setting up of Dearing's Inquiry. The time is indeed ripe to stand back and debate the future of higher education.

Adrian Seville's paper provides vivid and useful insights into one particular aspect of this debate. He shows how the option of 'strong' modularisation could go some way to alleviating the funding crisis, and would introduce 'quasi'-market mechanisms into higher education. Like many of the nationalised industries of old, the producer-driven higher education industry as it currently stands suffers from inefficiencies and lack of responsiveness to its consumers; Seville points out how modularisation could ameliorate some of these problems.

Seville's paper is particularly valuable because it challenges many of the assumptions concerning higher education. It explores fundamental issues such as the nature of a degree, and goes back to first principles over funding arrangements. Moreover, he is willing to challenge whether the current quality control mechanisms in higher education – brought into doubt only by moves towards flexibility and diversity – can be considered at all satisfactory even in a traditional university setting. But there remains a fundamental assumption within his paper which needs to be examined: why is it assumed that government should be involved in higher education at all? Seville explicitly states that he is not going to question that government funding is necessary 'for a developed nation' (p. 63); moreover, although he is sceptical about the viability of the alternative quality control mechanisms which he puts forward, he does not want to give up the notion that government has a rightful and justified place in being involved in such regulation.

Seville is not alone in making these assumptions. The vast majority of recent contributions on the future of higher education, which ostensibly have set out to go back to first principles, which have been willing to question almost everything else, have balked at questioning whether there is a role for the state in the funding, provision and regulation of higher education (for example, Barnett, 1990, MacIntyre, 1990, Feinberg, 1989, and Mendus, 1992). In this critical introduction, I challenge this lacuna in the literature. What are the justifications that could be given for the state to intervene in higher education?

Interestingly, the Dearing Committee did briefly consider why government is involved in the funding of higher education. But only one of the four reasons produced has any possible validity, while the other three reveal their misplaced faith in government solutions. *First*, they say that the government has 'a direct interest in ensuring that participation in the UK matches that of its competitors' (NCIHE, 1997, para. 91). This assumes that there is direct causal relation between such participation and a competitive economy, which a cursory glance at any of the published figures will reveal as nonsense. Is Greece, with 28·9 per cent of its 18-21 year olds enrolled in university really more competitive than Germany with 8·7 per cent? (OECD, 1996).

Second, government needs to intervene to ensure that 'tomorrow's workforce' is properly equipped for the demands of future technology and competition, and, *third*, because 'it needs to secure the economic and cultural benefits which higher education can offer the whole nation' (NCIHE, 1997, para. 91). At the IEA, Sir Ron Dearing told us an anecdote of how the Robbins Committee in the 1960s was sure that the *microfiche* was the tool of the future, with which every student needed to be properly familiar. The insight of this anecdote is apparently lost on him. For the problem with predicting the economic future is that governments are notoriously bad at it. But the market has evolved as a mechanism for coping with this uncertainty, by allowing the devolved knowledge and preferences of individuals to interact in the spontaneous order. Markets can respond to 'new challenges...which we cannot foresee from the perspective of 1997', as Dearing put it (*ibid.*, para. 128), but government cannot. As for preserving the culture of the nation, is Dearing not aware of the critique which suggests that there is an enormous undermining of culture taking place in our universities, under the guise of post-modern fashion, fostered by the cosy relationship academics have with the state?

Finally, there is one reason with any possible validity: government must intervene to 'ensure that access to opportunities for individuals to benefit from higher education is socially just' (*ibid.*, para. 91). This is a reason to which we return later in this introductory chapter. It may indeed be justification for a small rôle for state intervention in higher education, but certainly does not justify the huge gamut of funding and regulation with which we are familiar, and which, incidentally, Dearing is proposing to increase.

Seville's paper can of course stand alone – those who are interested in exploring the debate about modularisation do not *have* to consider this further question of whether genuine, rather than 'quasi-' market mechanisms can be brought to bear on higher education. Without this discussion, Seville's paper remains a valuable contribution to that debate, revealing how the present system can be modified to make it more responsive to customer demand. The discussion of Dearing's Review of Higher Education can continue, too, without any probing of these fundamental issues. But, for authors of Institute of Economic Affairs papers at least, any discussion of 'quasi'-markets begs the question as to why not 'genuine' or 'more authentic' markets? The debate about the future of higher education can be infused with a richer understanding if put into the broader context of why state intervention in higher education is justified at all. Hence the presence of this critical introduction which provides an overview of some of the arguments.

We begin by considering the nature of higher education, and the ways in which government can be involved, before exploring three justifications which could be given for state intervention in higher education. To anticipate the conclusion, we suggest that none is convincing, and that such state intervention cannot be justified.

What is Higher Education?

There are two aspects to 'Higher Education', or, as it used to be known, 'the advancement of learning', which are worth distinguishing for the purposes of this essay. *First*, there is the pushing forward of the frontiers of *human* knowledge, skill and understanding, defined here as the *'research'* component. *Second*, there is the pushing forward of the frontiers of *an individual's* knowledge, skill and understanding. This I call the *'higher learning'* component of higher education – understood, as Barnett (1990, p. 152) points out, to encompass both the learning of new material and critical evaluation of what is learnt. Some might argue that a third important part of 'higher education' is 'teaching'. I have not included this, however, because, I suggest, teaching is neither a necessary nor a sufficient condition for higher education to take place. (Clearly, research can take place without any teaching, and vice versa. But although higher learning may take place through teaching, it can also take place autodidactically, or through a common 'seminar' learning process, and so on. Similarly, teaching ostensibly for the purposes of higher education can take place and no higher learning result.)

Government Intervention in Higher Education

Government intervention in higher education can be in the form of regulation, provision and funding (Barr, 1993, p. 80). Government can regulate the supply side (for example, through Royal Charters, the Research Assessment Exercise, Higher Education Funding Council quality control measures, and so on) and the demand side (for instance, through allocating students to courses). Intervention in provision involves the government itself producing the goods and services (for example, by building, funding and employing lecturers). Finally, state intervention in funding can be either direct or indirect – the former involving direct government subsidy (or taxation) of the price of the good, while the latter involves transfers to individuals (funded places to be taken up at any university).

In the current system, government intervenes in all three ways. However, all three are independent – just because government is involved in one, does not mean that it has to be involved in the others (although it is unlikely that there could ever be much funding without regulation in a democracy, because of the demand for accountability).

Format of the Paper

Given this framework, I suggest that the following three justifications would be given for state intervention in higher education. Without state intervention:

1. There would not be higher education – research and higher learning – opportunities available at all.

2. There would not be *particular sorts of* higher education – research and higher learning – opportunities available (for example, advancement of learning for technological superiority in war or in commerce; advancement of learning in the arts and humanities).

3. There would not be equity in terms of access to higher learning.

The first two arguments can be explored by looking at historical and economic arguments, and are the subject of Chapter 2. The third demands some philosophical exploration of what is meant by equity and whether government can deliver it in higher education, the subject of Chapter 3.

2 | Justifications for State Intervention in Higher Education

Without the State, no Higher Education Opportunities?

Sceptics of the potential for higher education without the state could perhaps be persuaded by the demonstration that, in one nation at least, higher education evolved without state funding and provision, and with only minimal regulation. An even more convincing case could be made if it could be shown that, in that nation, although the state gradually did take over funding and provision and imposed greater regulation, such intervention was not needed for educational ends. I believe such a case can be made for the evolution of higher education in England and Wales.

In my experience, it is sobering to discover how many students, when probed about the growth of higher education in England and Wales, simply assume that government intervention was needed to get higher education underway, apart perhaps from the exceptions of Oxford and Cambridge. This is far from the truth. Government intervention in higher education consisted only of the minor regulations allowing for the registration of Royal Charters until 100 years ago, and then any funding and regulation were minimal until after the Second World War.

The 'Advancement of Learning' as a Charitable Activity

From the Tudor period right through to 1919, 'the advancement of learning' was regarded 'as an activity which was not the responsibility of the state but of the private citizen' (Shattock, 1994, p. 99). Indeed, the authoritative statement of what comprised 'charitable giving' came from Romilly in 1805, where one of the four objects of charity was 'the advancement of learning'.[1] The first colleges at Oxford

---

[1] In the Statute of Charitable Uses of 1601, the universities were identified as 'eleemosynary' ('charitable', *Oxford English Dictionary*) corporations, along with cathedrals, collegiate churches, Eton, Westminster and

and Cambridge, as is well known, evolved out of the monastic halls, training scholars for the ecclesiastical hierarchy. In the 16th and 17th centuries, the religious sponsors were replaced by prominent lay people, with new colleges completely endowed through the gifts of wealthy benefactors:

> By the nineteenth century, the colleges possessed considerable landed wealth and substantial invested capital and were fully able, with the support of endowed fellowships, scholarship schemes and so forth to support a student population which ranged from the very wealthy to the very poor. (Shattock, 1990, p. 99)

It was similarly the case with the new civic universities of the 19th century. My own university, Manchester, was named after its founder as Owens College. John Owens donated £100,000 to found it, and 90 per cent of the remaining £300,000 initial endowment came from individuals (merchants, manufacturers, engineers and lawyers), with only 10 per cent from business and other organisations. A similar variety of large- and small-scale philanthropy funded the universities of Liverpool, Leeds, Birmingham, Sheffield, Bristol, Hull, Nottingham, Reading, Southampton, and the University of Wales. Note how it was civic and – in the latter case, national – pride which in part prompted these donors, as well as a normal philanthropic interest in self-aggrandisement coupled with concern for the disadvantaged. Let us be clear: these institutions were opened and initially flourished without any state funding or provision, and with only the minor regulations accompanying registration for their Royal Charter.

Even if the institutions were established through philanthropy, this is a far cry from saying that they could survive financially over the long term – and we would need the latter conclusion to suppose that higher education without the state was financially viable. The received wisdom is that the universities found it hard to 'keep their heads above water' on the basis of these private donations alone. It was not until 1889, however, that government became involved in

---

Winchester. Their special position remains under all subsequent legislation, including the Charities Act of 1960.

giving grants to the universities.[2] Again, received wisdom is that this was because by this time 'their condition could no longer be ignored'. The grants thus provided 'represented a life-line for some institutions, and saved at least one, Sheffield, from bankruptcy' (Shattock, 1994, p. 102). If so, it might be argued that it is clear that the universities could not survive without government funding, and hence that such intervention was and is still needed.

However, *two* points need to be made about this. *First*, these grants were very small, and were explicitly intended only to 'assist in making up a deficiency which arose from the failure of endowment and fees to cover the colleges' recurrent costs' (p. 102) – so there was no question even then of government meeting all costs of higher education. *Second*, was it right that government should intervene in this way, to save, for example, Sheffield University from bankruptcy? Presumably, it is not generally assumed that government is right to save each and every failing business. Some become obsolete, or inefficient, and competition is needed to ensure that the inefficient are weeded out, and technological innovation introduced. So there may just have been too many institutions of higher education even in the 19th century – after all, civic (or national) pride may not be the best guide to the demand for a university in any particular town (or country). Sheffield, for example, is close to both Manchester and Leeds – perhaps these universities were satisfying the same market more efficiently? But this then raises perhaps the most crucial question: why did government intervene in the universities at that time?

Without the State, *Particular Sorts* of Higher Education not Provided?

The answer lies in the second justification for state intervention in higher education, that without state intervention, there will be market failure in delivering particular desired kinds of higher education. In 19th century England and Wales, the kind of higher education desired, and that was feared not being delivered in the market, was higher

---

[2] Except that there were, from 1832, small annual grants to the University of London (later University College) for its external examining role, and an *ad hoc* grant to assist the University of Wales.

education for technological competitiveness. This is a familiar theme today, as well as fears that the opposite is true, that increasing 'marketisation' of higher education would lead to the demise of the humanities and the arts. Let us look at the historical evidence briefly from the 19th and 20th centuries first, before considering the notion more generally from an economic perspective.

From the late 1860s, the fear was that Britain was losing its technological edge against France, the USA, and, in particular, Germany. Hence government intervention was needed in order to rectify this, and in particular, this meant intervention in higher education (as well as in primary and secondary education). A key factor in creating this public impression was the efforts of Lyon Playfair, a chemistry professor, who was one of the English jurors at the Paris Exhibition of 1867. He was instrumental in drawing parliamentary and public attention to the fact that the British were now lagging in technological capability behind the other Europeans, in particular the Germans, responsibility for which he ascribed to their more efficient schools and universities.

However, other sources suggest that Britain was not even then hampered by a lack of scientific skills and knowledge (for example, Habakkuk, 1962, p. 216): 'The relative decline in economic progress was more attributable to long-term changes in market opportunities which were in turn partly due to England's early start in industrialisation.' (West, 1970, p. 107) Moreover, on particular issues which exercised Playfair, other factors could account for the deficiencies. For example, concerning the scientific advances in the German steel industry, it was the invention of an Englishman, not a German, which made these advances possible: Sidney Gilchrist Thomas, an English police court clerk and amateur scientist, who conducted his experiments in his suburban garden, discovered the process by which to make steel out of phosphoric ore in 1875: 'The Germans were able to use the invention not because they were more foresighted or had impressive state schools but simply because the invention enabled them at last to exploit their own ores, which were phosphoric.' (p. 108)

The point of these accounts is to suggest that the reason why government initially became involved to 'save British universities' in the late 19th century was because of the perception that they were not enabling Britain to compete technologically, that there was market failure in this area. However, even accepting that universities should have this role, we see that the market failure was more imagined than real. Both abstractly, and concretely, it does not seem that an easy argument can be made for the need and justification for state intervention in higher education in the late 19th century in England and Wales. Indeed, similar arguments can be made as we follow the course of state intervention in higher education.

War and the Expansion of Higher Education Control

The First World War brought about state intervention in higher education in the UK in earnest, first with the establishment of the Department of Scientific and Industrial Research (DSIR) in 1915 which became the University Grants Committee in 1919, a new permanent committee under the Treasury.[3] But it is also true that, even though the state saw university funding as being of tremendous importance right up to the start of the Second World War, government (local and national) funding of higher education in England and Wales represented at most about 40 per cent of total income, with the remaining 60 per cent coming from private sources.[4] The advancement of learning was still primarily privately funded, and the universities still 'retained the essentially

---

[3] Oddly, Shattock comments that such state funding freed universities from the pressures of private benefactors guiding research: 'The problem of reliance on private benefactions and low fees was the potential it offered for the aims of the institution to be distorted by the whims of donors.... The injection of state funding, therefore, had the effect of removing an absolute dependence on pressures exerted by private donors.' (Shattock, 1994, p. 104) But this is surely a case of 'out-of-the-frying pan, into the fire', for is it not better to have funds from a variety of sources, some of whose pressure can be resisted, than from a monopoly source whose pressure cannot legally be resisted?

[4] Between 1920-21 and 1938-39, UGC recurrent grant was about 30 per cent of total university income, endowments and donations rose in that period from 13 to 18 per cent; student fees were 32 per cent in 1920, and examination fees 7 per cent; by 1938-39, these combined were 30 per cent (probably reflecting the recession) – but still roughly the same as the UGC contribution. Local authorities contributed about 9 per cent of income (Shattock, 1994, p. 106).

private characteristics which reflected their origins' (Shattock, 1994, p. 106).

The Second World War again brought considerable further government involvement. However, if we consider the reasons given for the state to take over responsibility for funding *after* the Second World War, most if not all were temporary problems caused by the disruption of the war. It was argued by contemporary sources that state aid to the universities was needed, for

> 'where else is the money to come from? Not from local authorities ... Not from private benefactors, crippled by Income Tax, Surtax, Excess Profits Tax, Capital Levy and Death Duties. Not from fees ... Only State aid is left; and only the State has aid available on the scale that is needed.' (Truscot, writing in 1945, quoted in Shattock, 1994, p. 107.)

Hence, state intervention in university funding was required because of the ravages of war, something which presumably could be considered only a temporary expedient.

New funding, however, brought new regulation, and new vested interests with expectations of continuing state funding: in 1946, the UGC reconstituted with new terms of reference, enlarging its functions to take over a planning role over universities. During the period from 1946 to 1979, the state gradually took over responsibility for full funding of the universities. But even in the 1960s, the Robbins Committee paid great tribute to the importance of private funds, expressing concern that 'the predominance of state funding could act as a deterrent to private benefactions' (p. 105). There was also concern that Treasury-imposed rules 'prohibiting the mixing of public and private funds in capital building projects imposed restrictions on institutional initiative' (pp. 105-06).

Robbins's Hidden Agenda

For many, the Robbins Report will be seen as the nail in the coffin of any argument which purports to show that state intervention in higher education is not needed, whatever arguments may have applied earlier this century, or late in the last. For it is surely indisputable that the Committee on Higher Education, set up by the Government in the early 1960s, was a thoroughly reputable body, which carefully explored all the issues, and concluded, most definitely, that further state intervention was decidedly urgent, for the sake of education and British competitiveness.

However, a careful reading of the Robbins Report could lead one to alternative conclusions. For it seems that it could have been the prejudices and predilections of the Committee on Higher Education which determined the famous Robbins Report conclusions, not the evidence reviewed.

A clear example of this can be found when we see how conclusions were drawn from the evidence submitted on international comparisons – crucial to the final recommendations.

Robbins's sentiments are well known: 'the conclusion is plain ... Both in general cultural standards and in competitive intellectual power, vigorous action is needed to avert the danger of a serious relative decline in this country's standing' (Committee on Higher Education, 1963a, para. 130). The only way to resolve Britain's deleterious relative position with its competitors was by a great expansion of higher education, an expansion involving additional public spending.

However, when the evidence presented to the Committee is reviewed – *even looking at this evidence in terms of Robbins's own summary* – it is hard to see how this conclusion could possibly be sustained. The Robbins Committee, it seems, was highly selective in its use of comparative statistics. Far more plausible conclusions would be:

1. There is no established connection between economic and social development and higher education – and the case of Germany warrants particular attention in this regard;

2. Great Britain was doing particularly well in relation to its European competitors, and, at most, some temporary expansion was needed to cater for the 'post-war bulge'; and

3. Where Britain fell short by comparison with the USA was in the lack of private finance in higher education.

How are these contrary conclusions arrived at? *First*, consider the numbers entering higher education. The evidence is presented and the conclusion drawn that 'the British system came some way down that list' (para. 123). True, out of seven countries reviewed, Britain came fifth. However, this could be construed as a rather misleading way of reading the statistics, for Great Britain with 4·5 per cent of the relevant population entering higher education was higher than Germany (4 per cent) – surely of significance? – and the Netherlands (3 per cent), and roughly comparable with the USSR (5 per cent) – and it is the USSR in particular which is highly praised later. Britain's entry figures are only inferior to France's (7 per cent), Sweden's (10 per cent) and the USA's (20 per cent). So another way of putting this conclusion might have been that 'the British system does not compare unfavourably as far as entry figures are concerned'. Robbins's hidden agenda is beginning to emerge.

Second, as Britain had a much lower wastage rate than other countries, *graduation* rates are particularly important to examine. With these, Britain came out far better, at 5.6 per cent of the relevant age group, almost twice as high as France and Germany (3 per cent), roughly the same as Sweden (6 per cent), and not very far behind the USSR (7 per cent). (No figures were available for the USA.) These figures would presumably lead the Committee to trumpet the achievements of the British system? Not a bit of it. They immediately dampened any enthusiasm that might be kindled in a reader by pointing out that, never mind the favourable comparisons with Western Europe, 'the output of British higher education is, in very important respects, smaller than that of the Soviet Union or the United States' (para. 126). And it is this comparison which steals the day. Even though it is admitted that 'There may be much dispute about the standard of some first degrees in the United States' (para. 126), this does not seem to matter: 'undeniably', a much greater proportion of Americans get degrees.

In case there should still be any doubt, the Report adds: 'the total advantage of higher education to a country or to its people cannot be fully described in terms of the numbers who successfully complete it. Those who abandon higher education in other countries may yet be more useful citizens in the community on account of their experience' (para. 126). Perhaps they will be. But perhaps disillusioned young people, out of the labour market for three or more years in a failed attempt to get a degree, having incurred loans and foregone earnings, might also be rather less useful citizens 'on account of their experience'. Robbins does not consider this possibility, and the suspicion is that it is an *ad hoc* rationalisation, to continue to undermine the British system.

This discussion reveals two of Robbins's great passions: the higher education systems in the USA and USSR. (His third was for central planning of any kind – for see how he gushes about France and Sweden, even when, in both countries, he agrees that central planning has not been successful, or might not bring any tangible results.)[5] It also reveals his decision to avoid the uncomfortable anomaly of the Federal Republic of Germany.

Curiously, the Report does not mention the German anomaly at all, and to gauge its significance the Appendices to the report have to be consulted. There, it is first noted that in Germany, there will not be any expansion of higher education in the 1960s, partly because their 'baby boom' was in the 1930s not the 1940s, so expansion had already taken place. Moreover, in Germany there was no sign of an increase in 'the proportion of the age group completing a secondary education in the *Gymnasien* (grammar schools) and obtaining the qualifications for university entrance' (Committee on Higher Education, 1963b). This proportion was already lower than in Great Britain and France. It is further noted:

> This is most surprising in view of the recent economic growth of Germany, for in most western countries prosperity is thought to be a main reason why a steadily increasing proportion of young people desire to complete secondary education and proceed to further study. (Committee on Higher Education, 1963b, p. 80)

If in one of the important growing economies of Western Europe, higher education is not a cause, or even an effect, of this growth, that is an important anomaly worth reporting and analysing for its significance. The Report touches on reasons for a paragraph or so, pointing out that 'education in Germany is not so consciously recognised as the ladder of

---

[5] 'It is not so much the present state of educational affairs in France that has significance for Great Britain ... as the imaginative plans adopted for the future. To say that there is a possibility that the situation in 1970 will in certain respects fall short of the French Government's current plans is not to detract from the importance of the fact that these plans now exist, and that steps are being taken to put them into effect' (Committee on Higher Education, 1963a, p. 57).

social advancement...and there are also long memories of graduate unemployment in the past' (p. 80). But rather than explore this in any more depth, that is the end of it. And when in the Report they explore the connection between economic and social development and higher education they do not even mention this counter-example.

What of Robbins's passion for the USSR and the USA? Perhaps we do not need to spend any time on the Soviet Union, for not only were the official statistics rather more suspect than others, we also might baulk at the social costs imposed by that régime, whatever they were able to do in terms of higher education expansion. So we focus only on the comparison between the USA and Great Britain. Let us ignore the admitted (by Robbins) questionable quality of degrees in the USA. What was the single most important difference between the higher education systems in these two countries? In the evidence given to the Robbins Committee it was surely private finance.

With regard to public expenditure on higher education, Britain *spent the (equal) greatest proportion of GNP* of all the countries reviewed: 1962-3 figures showed Britain, with 0·8 per cent of GNP spent on higher education, equal to the USA and USSR, and much greater than France (0·3 per cent), Germany (0·4 per cent) and Sweden (0·5 per cent). Where Britain fell short, particularly in comparison with North America, was in terms of *private* expenditure. By this time, only 10 per cent of all higher education expenditure in Britain was from private sources, compared to 31 per cent in the USA.

This fact is only mentioned in passing in the report (Committee on Higher Education, 1963a, p. 45), and *ignored completely* when finance is considered, and recommendations made. Presumably it offended Robbins's notion of what a higher education system should be, even though the evidence begs for it to be considered.

What is being suggested is that the initial state intervention was not justified, nor was Robbins's expansion. But all this begins to build up a picture of unnecessary intervention all the way through. The foundations of justified state intervention in higher education are beginning to crumble.

Externalities of Higher Education

We can place this discussion in the context of more general economic arguments which concern whether state intervention in higher education is needed because of *externalities*; indeed, in economics textbooks, this would often be the primary reason why the state should intervene in higher education.[6] *Externalities* exist when one person's or group's self-interested action affects the utility of some other person or group. In terms of this argument concerning higher education, when individuals educate themselves, or pursue their own research agendas, they have the potential to benefit not only themselves, but the whole of society. (For example, Sidney Gilchrist Thomas pursuing his scientific interests indirectly leading to benefits to a whole nation.) The market failure argument is that, in this case, the economic and technological needs of society will not be catered for by people pursuing their own ends in this way. There are external benefits which individuals cannot capture for themselves so there will be less investment in education than is optimal for society unless government provides a subsidy.

However, there are several difficulties with the externality argument. *First*, the proposition that increased human capital is beneficial in causing economic expansion generally may be true. But, as Milton Friedman has pointed out, we could make the identical proposition concerning physical capital too. If the externality argument can be used to justify state funding for higher education, it could also be used to justify state subsidy of investment in buildings and machinery in, say, Vauxhall Motors (Friedman, 1962). *Second*, there is the difficulty that no-one has yet come up with a satisfactory way of measuring these externalities empirically, so it is hard to know how the size of the required subsidy could be calculated. *Third*, suppose that the case for net positive externalities *could* be made. Then, as West points out, there would still not be a clear case for government intervention. For suppose that a

---

[6] The 'information problem' would be the other key economic reason why states should intervene in education generally (see, for example, Barr, 1993); however, as Barr agrees, it seems more difficult for this argument to be applied to *higher* education. For in this case, the 'consumers' are now young adults, and so a protection-of-minors principle does not need to be evoked to prevent ignorant choosers jeopardising the education of a third party. We touch on this at the end of Chapter 3.

government-funded and provided university was to provide £X of higher education per person. Prior to this government intervention, some families or individuals would already be providing more than £X, others less than £X, some none. The last two groups would clearly benefit from this intervention (providing, of course, that quality was ensured). But the first group, or some members, might be tempted to opt for £X level for free, rather than pay for greater than £X. This action would then have a downward effect on total educational expenditure (West, 1995, p. 142).

Negative Externalities of Government Intervention in Higher Education

Finally, it may be that there are *negative* externalities of government intervention in higher education too (although the problem of measurement also reappears for these). These could include 'social unrest among a highly educated, yet significantly unemployed, intelligentsia' (West, 1995, p. 142), and the related issue of 'qualification inflation'. Let us look at the latter in more detail, for it challenges many of the assumptions which seem to prevail around the current expansion of higher education in the UK, as well as the earlier expansion in the 1960s. The almost universal consensus seems to be that the more young people who can be brought into higher education, the better it is for Britain and the young people. But there is evidence which should disturb this consensus: if the expansion of higher education simply means that more and more young people have degrees, so increasing numbers of jobs require graduates rather than lower-level qualifications, then it may be that no-one is better off than before the expansion started. Ronald Dore, in the *Diploma Disease*, summed up the problem well over 20 years ago. One of his examples was of librarianship:

> At the beginning of the century a librarian had to have only a 'love of books and the capacity to advise the managers as to purchases and inquirers as to suitable works' – he had, in other words, actually to be able to do his job. By the 1930s intending librarians were told that a school certificate was a 'useful possession'. By 1950 it was the minimal requirement. ... By 1970 two A levels [were required]... (Dore, 1976, p. 24).

Today of course the requirement is at least a degree, preferably in 'information science', and probably a Master's degree too. But employers of librarians are not being irrational in seeking these higher qualifications even though the demands of the job are no harder (presumably much easier with the advent of information technology):

> Fifty years ago, large numbers of people who were bright enough to be good librarians left school before the age of 15, and most of those who continued their education beyond the age of 15 had access to better paid or more prestigeful jobs than librarianship. Nowadays, by contrast, most of the children who have the required level of librarian potential stay on at school until the age of 18. (Moreover, the big expansion of numbers staying at school until the age of 18 means that they cannot all, as perhaps they could fifty years ago, expect *more* rewarding jobs than librarianship.) Hence libraries *can get* people with higher level certificates; and they *need to* recruit such people if they are to go on recruiting men and women with the same degree of librarian potential as those they were recruiting fifty years earlier. (p. 26)

The suggestion is that the extra schooling being obtained by these people is *not relevant* to their careers as librarians. It is simply to compete in the positional goods competition that they stay on in schooling. Recent statistics from the UK illustrate this process quite graphically. For example, the Institute for Employment Studies' (1996) report, *What Do Graduates Really Do?*, followed three cohorts of graduates from one university. It revealed an astonishing level of graduate 'underemployment'. Less than half of the graduates considered that the employment they had achieved up to three years after graduation required 'graduate level ability', while one in 10 reported that they were in a job which they knew had previously been held by a school leaver. Indeed, one-fifth of humanities graduates was in clerical or secretarial work. Overall, three-fifths of graduates reported that they thought they were underemployed in their work, lacking intellectual challenge, or doing tasks which required little skill or knowledge, and certainly not the skills learned in their degree.

Similar results have been reported over the years. The 1990 government report, *Highly Qualified People: Supply and Demand*, showed that 'Britain already has considerably more in the way of highly qualified labour than it can absorb in any capacity' – and that was before the current upsurge in higher education recruitment (Murphy, 1991, p. 241). That survey had revealed that two-thirds of jobs employing new graduates could have been done equally well by school leavers or people with work experience. Employers had reported that they were not demanding any more from their new graduate recruits than they had from previous non-graduates. Disturbingly, these reports more or less reiterate what the Robbins Report had said almost 30 years earlier – that even a fifth of scientists and technologists were 'in categories of employment in which it is unlikely they were making full use of their qualifications' (Committee on Higher Education, 1963a).

In general, then, 'qualification inflation' is when higher and higher qualifications are needed for a particular job, *even though the actual demands of the job are not getting any greater*.

This may seem a sad fact of the positional goods problem, but why is it suggested that this could be a negative consequence (externality) of *government* intervention? The problem, of course, is that it is *government intervention* which is subsidising the expansion of young people going through higher education.[7] If university education was not heavily subsidised or free (as it has been in the UK) at the point of delivery, together with a heavily subsidised, and, it must be said, rather pleasant lifestyle, fewer young people would bother getting it, and hence the supply-side spiral of higher credentials offered, coupled with the employer-led demand-side spiral of higher credentials demanded, would not be such a problem. Dore summarises his findings from developed and developing countries alike: 'It is not a bad generalisation that the almightiness of the certificate varies in direct proportion to the predominance of the state in the development process' (Dore, 1976, p. 74).

Of course, it might be thought that this raises an important equity issue, that without government sponsored qualification inflation, the rich would be particularly rewarded. We shall see in Chapter 2 below, there is a solution to this equity problem which could make everyone aware of the real costs of higher education, but not discourage those who could genuinely benefit from pursuing it.

---

[7] Also government sanctioning of 'closed shop' measures by professional bodies to prohibit entrants to their careers without degrees or higher qualifications (see Tooley, 1995b).

No Need for State Intervention in Higher Education

We have suggested, using historical and economic arguments, that state intervention in higher education was not necessary. The example of England and Wales is a counter-example to the claim that state intervention in funding and provision is needed, either in order to bring about higher education in the first place or to ensure that higher education for success in terms of economic and technological competitiveness is provided. It is suggested that none of the earlier interventions in higher education could be justified on the grounds given for them, with the exception perhaps of those after the Second World War. But just because the war-damaged economy required state intervention in the universities does not mean that such intervention is still required later on. Even the Robbins Report, which is taken by many as showing the need for greater state intervention in higher education, does not seem to have its trenchant conclusions to this effect supported by the evidence. Abstractly, too, the discussion of externalities has questioned the power of these arguments to show that, without government intervention, particular types of market failure will arise; indeed, it seems likely that there are significant negative externalities of government intervention in higher education.

Could these arguments still be applicable today? Without the state intervening in funding, provision and regulation of universities, would the advancement of learning take place? It is hard to see why not. Of course, there is huge technological advancement, and tremendous competition from overseas. But why would individuals not see it in their interests to gain degrees in the subjects which are needed for that advancement – in technology, science, engineering, for example? The real after-tax private rate of return to an individual for university education is estimated to be very high – estimated at 10 per cent in Canada (West, 1995, p. 135), so why would such a reward not be individually desirable.

Perhaps the complaint would be, as noted earlier, that 'liberal' learning would suffer, that there would be market failure in the advancement of learning in, say, the arts or humanities. As Barr points out, if this was a real risk, then it could be assuaged by having state vouchers tied to those particular subjects which may need protecting in the market – not accountancy, law or economics, but perhaps the classics, music, etc. (Barr, 1993). However, even this perhaps assumes too much. It is not in the private schools in England and Wales, for example, that the classics have been eliminated, but in state schools. The proposition that there would not be the elements of a liberal education on offer without state intervention assumes, *first*, that there would be no philanthropists who thought it worth funding others to do these pursuits, or, *second*, that there would not be those who thought it worth pursuing these subjects themselves in their own time, or for modest remuneration. It is not clear from where such assumptions arrive.

It may be that, without state intervention in the funding of certain humanities, such as philosophy, there would not be as many people studying them full-time as there are at present. But to argue that this proves that state intervention is necessary assumes that there is an optimum figure for the number of people studying these subjects, which is known by the state, and could be achieved by state intervention. Again, it is not clear how anyone could argue such a position. The issue of equity can, however, be raised – the third justification for state intervention in higher education. If fewer people are able to study these disciplines without the state, then others are being deprived of that opportunity. The equity issue is the subject of the next chapter.

3 | Equity and Social Justice

Without the state, it is argued, there would not be equity in terms of access to higher learning. In this paper, we will not spend time analysing what is meant by equity in too much depth (for more details see Tooley, 1995a, 1996). Let us take a rough-and-ready notion that equity in higher learning could be arrived at when access is extended to all – so that all who wish to partake of higher education are able to do so. For present purposes, we are thinking rather narrowly of 'access to higher education' as meaning access to the institutions of universities, etc., in other words, accepting something like the *status quo*. With the ideas in Chapter 4 below, or those brought out in Seville's accompanying paper, it may well emerge that access to higher education would be far less expensive and exclusive, when the state's grip on higher education is lessened. Hence the problem of access may be far less of an issue. But for now, let us keep with the *status quo* and see what emerges.

Equity and Entrance Requirements

One complication is that there may be entrance requirements set on those who are able to attend higher education establishments which in practice 'discriminate' against lower socio-economic groups, in the sense that fewer from these groups are able to achieve these requirements. Some would argue that this is in itself undermining equity.

An argument could be constructed to suggest that it would not be so. This would hinge upon whether some people have a particular *aptitude* for higher education, which can be measured in some way, such as through IQ tests and scholastic examinations. If it was accepted that such an aptitude did exist, then even radical egalitarian philosophies would not seem to be offended by only such people being given the opportunity to attend institutions of higher education. For example, a Rawlsian model allows there to be inequalities of opportunity in society if these further the position of the worst off in society (Rawls, 1972). But it could easily be argued that allowing access to those, and *only* to those, who have the aptitude for higher education *would* benefit the whole of society, and particularly those worst off. Allocating higher education to such people would enable wealth to be effectively created, health to be effectively maintained, and so on. Hence such benefits would be available to be distributed for the benefit of the worst off. But conversely, allocating the scarce resources of higher education to those who would not be able to make the best use of them would bring less desirable results.

Similarly, the even more radically egalitarian Dworkin also tolerates inequalities in society with his 'equality of resources' model.[1] For if individuals have contributed much to the community, then Dworkin says they are entitled to take more out of the common pot. But then this is consistent with arguing that those who *are objectively likely to* contribute more once they have had their higher education should be given 'more out of the common pot', in order to give them the opportunity to contribute more. So even under these radical models, we can see how a 'meritocracy' in the distribution of access to higher education may emerge and hence allow, on the grounds of equity, particular selection procedures imposed on access to higher education. Again, when the ideas in Chapter 4 are taken into account, or if something like Seville's modularity model pertains, we may not need to embrace such selection procedures: that is, without (or with less rigid) state intervention, higher education may become far more flexible,

---

[1] Dworkin denies that equality implies anything like 'equality of result', that is, 'that citizens must each have the same wealth at every moment of their lives' (Dworkin, 1985, p. 206). What it requires is that people should *begin* life on an equal footing, or, failing that, that their 'market allocations must be corrected in order to bring [them] closer to the share of resources they would have had but for these various differences of initial advantage, luck, and inherent capacity' (p. 207). Treating people as equals requires a complex calculation be made along the following lines: Divide the total resources available to all between the number of people; let us call this amount x units. Each individual cannot now take from the resources *on balance* more than x units. This is Dworkin's equality of resources.

The 'on balance' is important: for if individuals have contributed much to the community, then Dworkin says they are entitled to take more out (p. 206). This has the interesting implication that economic inequalities, even extreme ones, can still be present even with Dworkin's equality of resources.

and the above assumption based on aptitude for higher education may become irrelevant.

Given the desire for equity in terms of extending access to all, the important question is: what degree of state intervention is required to meet this desire? Does it require the whole gamut of state funding, provision and regulation with which we are now familiar? There are two arguments against. The first points to the inequity of the current model of state intervention. The second shows an alternative which could satisfy equity with only minimal state intervention.

Inequity in State Intervention in Higher Education

First, there is a clear empirical picture emerging that the extensive state intervention in higher education with which we are familiar has *not* promoted equity. For the work of Professor Julian Le Grand (1987) and others has shown that the funding of higher education is a classic example of the way the welfare state 'actually benefit[s] the middle classes at least as much as the poor, and in many cases more than the poor' (p. 91). Le Grand found that the ratio of state higher education expenditure per person in the top fifth of the socio-economic spectrum to that per person in the bottom fifth is 5.4:1. That is, the middle classes receive five and half times more per person in university expenditure than the working classes.

Income-Contingent Loans for Greater Access to Higher Education

If the current system is unfair, is there a means by which equity could be satisfied? In fact, there is an alternative arrangement that has been on the table for some time, which it appear would satisfy equity, and which involves rather minimal state involvement. This is the 'income-contingent loan' route. These are loans taken out by students to cover maintenance and tuition fees (although the latter is not accepted by all proponents of the model), repaid with interest through the tax or national insurance system, when the borrower achieves some proportion of national average income. The idea of income-contingent loans in this country can be traced back to the 1960s, to a paper published by the Institute of Economic Affairs (Peacock and Wiseman, 1964). In turn, their chain of influence can be traced back to Milton

Friedman. Dearing – and the government – have now embraced the principle of these loans, even if they seek initially to apply them only at the margins.

In 'The Role of Government in Education' (1955), republished in his *Capitalism and Freedom* (1962), Friedman argued on grounds of equity and efficiency for income-contingent loans to finance 'vocational and professional schooling'. He wrote:

> Individuals should bear the costs of investment in themselves and receive the rewards. They should not be prevented by market imperfections from making the investment in human beings. A governmental body could offer to finance or help finance the training of any individual who could meet minimum quality standards. It would make available a limited sum per year for a specified number of years. The individual in return would agree to pay to the government in each future year a specified percentage of his earnings in excess of a specified sum ... This payment could easily be combined with payment of income tax and so involve a minimum of additional administrative expense. The base sum should be set equal to estimated average earnings without the specialized training. (p. 105)

Peacock and Wiseman translated these ideas into the British context, and applied them to any area of 'higher learning'. Thus government:

> sets up a fund from which any student accepted by an authorised institution of higher learning can borrow to meet his education costs. ... The loans would be available to meet any kind of educational or related expense. The borrowing student would be required to sign a contract agreeing that for each unit borrowed he would add to his income tax payments each year, up to retirement age, an amount equal to a specified percentage of his taxable income. (p. 37)

Although this sounds like a 'graduate tax' version of the income-contingent loan, the comments immediately following – that there should be provision for paying back the loan sooner and that higher earners should not be penalised – suggest they were veering towards the notion of the pure income-contingent loan, where the borrowing stops when the loan plus interest is repaid.

An underlying promise of the income-contingent loan is that there may be advantages in loan collection *through government agencies* rather than through commercial banks, because of the differing incentives to default. With any loan system, there is a significant number of people who will seek to evade repayment, if they think that they can get away with it. With a loan for higher education, the borrower is not pledging physical collateral, for example, a house, so he may be more tempted to default. If, to avoid this problem, as some have proposed, the banks are guaranteed by government the loan repayment if the borrower defaults, then this will mean there are few if any incentives for the bank to pursue the defaulter. However, if the loan is registered with the income tax or National Insurance authorities, then the only realistic way to default is to become a vagrant or to leave the country, and hence to forego lifetime social security benefits. This is the fundamental (deterrent) advantage that governments have over private markets: the costs imposed on defaulters are automatic and extremely large. So governments genuinely are in a position to reduce transaction costs, because of their access to superior information and administrative economies, as they 'have already invested large resources in establishing machinery for income tax assessment and collection. The marginal costs of using this machinery for educational loans collection should be relatively small' (West, 1995, p. 150).

Robbins and Income-Contingent Loans

Just as with Friedman's ideas, it is very important to note that the Peacock and Wiseman proposals were introduced as the best method of satisfying both equality of opportunity or equity without sacrificing efficiency: the proposals, they argued, 'would minimise the financial obstacles facing talented students, and ... they would significantly reduce the discriminations apparent in the present British system' (Peacock and Wiseman, 1964, p. 54). Of particular interest, Peacock and Wiseman gave evidence to the Robbins Committee, which ultimately came down against their ideas. The reasons are worth examining in more detail, for they say much about the acceptability of income-contingent loans as satisfying equity – even though this is not what Robbins concluded.

Robbins agreed that there were two powerful moral arguments in favour of income-contingent loans, concerning social justice and individual responsibility. Higher education generally brought the prospect of substantially higher earnings, so 'if finance is provided by outright subsidy from public funds ... a new position of privilege is created' (Committee on Higher Education, 1963a, para. 642). Moreover, a student financed by grants would be 'apt to take his privilege for granted', leading to 'the lack of any particular sense of obligation and need to work'. But loans would focus the attention of the student, making such a person 'all the keener to get the most out of what he is buying' (para. 643).

But against were three arguments which, curiously, outweighed these advantages. The *first* was that 'the connexion between higher education and individual earning power can be over-stressed. Not all forms of higher education produce a large earnings differential' (para. 643). But this ignored, of course, precisely the argument for *income-contingent*, rather than mortgage-type, loans! *Second*, Robbins argued that there would be 'social advantages of investment in higher education', so that society should indeed be paying. But, even if this was correct (and Robbins admitted that there was no way of knowing if there really was this return to society), it would only preclude loans covering *all* of tuition and maintenance. As Peacock and Wiseman pointed out, there would be a need only for *some contribution* from society, not a 100 per cent subsidy.

Finally, there were various practical objections: There would be 'great administrative difficulties' in securing repayment of loans (para. 645) – ignoring the evidence for the administrative ease with which income-contingent loans could be repaid through the tax system. But of most concern, and what, it was stressed, fundamentally clinched the argument, was that having debts would put some young people off higher education. This was particularly true for women, since clearly their 'eligibility for marriage ... would be diminished by the addition to their charms of what would be in effect a negative dowry' (para. 645).

Political incorrectness aside, this ignored the argument that income-contingent loans were put forward precisely to avoid these traps. Married women or men who did not reach average graduate earnings would *not* have been liable to repay. There would have been no problem should one partner wish to withdraw from the labour market, a fact curiously ignored by Robbins.

Privatised Income-Contingent Loans

We have suggested that (a) the current gamut of state intervention in higher education has not brought about equity, and (b) that there is a model of funding, using income-contingent loans paid back through the tax or national insurance schemes, which could satisfy equity. Moreover, the latter model can be achieved with only minimal state intervention. Government itself only has to be involved by using its existing mechanisms to collect loans. The loans themselves can be held by commercial banks, or could involve government selling debt to the private sector, using the method of 'securitisation', a technique widely used, for example, by credit card companies (Barr and Crawford, 1996).[2]

Securitisation has the advantages of being genuinely competitive, with tradeable assets. Barr and Crawford note a further interesting corollary of their scheme:

> The financial asset, being long term, would be of particular interest to pension funds. Student debt could, for example, be held by a miners' pension fund, benefiting retired miners whose pension would, in part, derive from the human capital of younger graduates, and also benefiting younger people by providing the

---

[2] We can illustrate these using the figure of £1 billion, the current Student Loan Company's (SLC) debts. Barr and Crawford offer two methods of securitisation. The first is for current public spending with no guarantee. The SLC would offer £1 billion of debt, and the private buyers will pay £800 million to buy the future income stream; the Treasury pays the SLC the shortfall of £200 million. The SLC then has £1 billion to lend to students. The total amount of debt could be sold in small chunks, say of £10 million, allowing smaller financial institutions to participate, making the sale more competitive. Bidders could include merchant banks, life insurance companies and pension funds. The SLC would offer funds once or twice a year. Bidding would be through sealed bids or by auction. This method costs the taxpayer a one-time annual expenditure of £200 million. The risk is totally transferred to the private sector. The second method would be for a limited guarantee. This time, the Treasury makes no cash payment, but offers a guarantee of the first £200 million of losses incurred in the portfolio. The market buys the debt for around £1 billion. Hence the government never has to pay more than £200 million, but may benefit if the loss is not so great. In this case, the SLC sells the debt to a single institution, as it is now attractive to one underwriter to buy the entire issue. The underwriter then sells to smaller institutions, possibly in chunks as small as £10,000.

loan capital which finances part of the costs of their higher education (p. 16).

In other words, the argument from equity only requires the state to use its already existing mechanisms to act as a loan collector, and, possibly, to sell student debt to the private sector: it does not require *any other intervention*.

The Information Problem

What about quality control? Surely government regulations would be needed? The information problem is that consumers face particular difficulties in becoming informed about educational services, and hence need government quality control mechanisms. I have tackled this argument in detail elsewhere in relation to primary and secondary education, and suggested that it does not hold there as a justification for state intervention in education (Tooley, 1996, Ch. 5). *First*, we can say that the information problem is such an issue in the *equity debate* when applied to children, because it relies on sometimes ignorant parents making decisions on behalf of their children, which could lead to considerable unfairness. This problem, clearly, does not apply in the case of higher education, as the users of higher education are themselves adults, so there is no paternalistic, or 'protection of minors' principle at stake (Barr, 1993).

Second, the basic argument of the information problem is that, even if it is true that it is difficult for parents to obtain and use information about schooling – more difficult than deciding if a pair of shoes fits, for example – *it is much more difficult for the state*. In particular, the kinds of information which the state requires tend to be those that are easily measurable, and an emphasis on them distorts the educational process. An exactly parallel case can be made for higher education. Indeed, Seville has in part made it for us, by describing the whole range of quality control mechanisms currently in place and their ineffectuality (see his Chapter 2, below). Moreover, he goes on to describe the parameters of a system which would need to be put into place to ensure national quality control, and although he baulks at saying it is impossibly complex, the suggestion here is that it is.

But the crucial question remains: why would we need such incredibly complex systems when, in other areas of our lives, we depend on market indicators such as brand names and price, as well as consumer information publications, to help us make judgements about quality? While higher education is complex, it is not clear that choices about it are different in kind from choices about other complex services in the market, such as computing or banking. And if the quality of these services can be maintained without a nationalised system, there do not seem to be any good arguments which suggest the educational case is any different (see Tooley, 1997).

4 | The Future of Higher Education: HE Without the State

Should governments intervene in the funding, provision or regulation of higher education? The argument has been that such intervention is neither justified nor necessary. Such intervention was not needed historically in England and Wales – either to get higher education going or to ensure that higher education of a particular desired kind was provided. Moreover, the general economic argument that education provides external benefits which merit government subsidy does not seem to hold. Indeed, government intervention has the particularly unpleasant consequence of bringing about the negative externality of qualification inflation. Even if the aim is equity, government intervention is not needed, except to use established systems to collect repayments on privatised income-contingent loans.

Given that government intervention is not justified and not necessary, we can contemplate a future of higher education without the state. It is not the place here to suggest a detailed programme which would bring this about, but two key reforms are clearly required. First, universities must be permitted to charge whatever student fees they desire; second, a system of income-contingent loans repayable through the tax or National Insurance system needs to be initiated. Both of these could help alleviate the funding crisis in which higher education currently finds itself, and could, in principle, enable universities to liberate themselves *entirely* from state funding (by raising a greater proportion of their income through student fees) and hence from the deleterious impact of state regulation.

As far as higher learning is concerned, the major benefit of the separation of higher education and the state will be that, as students now have to pay for higher education – albeit being able to pay back over their life-time through income-contingent loans – some of them will come to behave as concerned consumers. This is likely to have two important and beneficial impacts. *First*, it will encourage young people to take more seriously the decision about going to university and consider whether other options are preferable. In the longer term this will reduce qualification inflation, by breaking the supply-side spiral, and hence cutting in to the employer-led demand-side spiral too. Young people will realise that it may be in their interests to go into work rather than study; employers will realise that they do not have to use a degree as a proxy for other measures, such as general intelligence, leadership, character, age, and so on (Murphy, 1991).

Second, those who do decide to partake of higher learning opportunities will be anxious to ensure value for money – or at least, some of the consumers will, and in any such market, only some of the consumers need to be concerned in order to raise quality for all (Tooley, 1996). Questions will be raised, such as why degree courses are spread over a leisurely (in England and Wales) three years – the University of Buckingham's two-year degree courses are particularly interesting in this regard, as are the shorter length courses provided by for-profit universities such as De Vry's and the University of Phoenix in the USA (Sperling and Tucker, 1997). Poor quality lecturing will not be tolerated: indeed, it will become questionable whether lecturing is a cost-effective and useful way of getting information across, given the technological possibilities available, or simply given the potential benefits of seminars with genuine scholars. Such pressures will also raise questions about the nature of higher education, and its institutional base: separating higher education from the state is also likely to bring about a transformation in the types of institutions in which it is conducted. Just as Seville below foresees the 'disaggregation', and perhaps the 'de-institutionalisation' of higher education, given moves towards modularisation, so I foresee similar occurrences brought to bear by the pressures of consumer demand.

It is likely that research and higher learning will continue on the process of separation that seems to have begun already. There is no reason why higher learning need co-exist alongside research. Much research could better be conducted within industry, or in specialised research institutions, or in looser networks of consultants, funded by business, charities, and perhaps by government.[1]

Moreover, the potential for higher learning can be transformed. Seville sees the process of modularisation bringing opportunities outside traditional universities (below, Ch. 4), perhaps in colleges of further education, or in institutions the like of which we have not as yet seen. But the genuine market solution offers the potential for even more radical transformation, particularly with the advent of the technological possibilities of CD-ROMs and the Internet. Indeed, we may see the undermining of the professionalisation of academia, which arguably has been to the detriment of intellectual activity: we might perhaps see a partial return to the earlier ideal of the advancement of learning as a charitable activity, firmly embedded in civil society. It is not the place here to engage in detailed prediction (see Hague, 1991, for ideas based on similar principles to those discussed here); it *is* the place to point to the conclusion that government is not needed in higher education, and that without it, flexibility and innovation can be the hallmark of the higher education process.

Under current government pressures, universities have become, to paraphrase Clark Kerr, places where a bunch of government lackeys are brought together to do research, united only 'by a common grievance over parking' (Kerr, 1972, p. 20). The advancement of learning deserves more than that. It can have it, outside of the state.

---

[1] What of the arguments that teachers of higher education should be doing research? I follow Barnett: although 'every teacher has a professional obligation to understand the key conversations going on' in their relevant research community (Barnett, 1990, p. 130), this scholarship does not imply that everyone who is teaching should actually be doing research. But would not this mean that students will not be brought to the frontiers of knowledge? Scholars and teachers can be familiar with work up to the frontiers, without being engaged in true research itself: 'the responsibility of the teacher lies much more in having an intimate understanding of other academics' research and in being able to give an interpretation of it' (p. 131), than in actually having to conduct research.

References/Bibliography

Barnett, Ronald (1990): *The idea of higher education*, Buckingham: Society for Research into Higher Education/Open University.

Barr, Nicholas (1993): *The Economics of the Welfare State*, 2nd edition, London: Weidenfeld and Nicolson.

Barr, Nicholas, and Crawford, Iain (1996): *Student loans: where are we now?*, London: LSE, Welfare State Programme, WSP/127.

Committee on Higher Education (1963a): *Higher Education: Report*, London: HMSO, Cmnd. 2154.

Committee on Higher Education (1963b): *Higher Education: Appendix Five: higher education in other countries*, London: HMSO.

Dore, Ronald (1976): *The Diploma Disease*, London: George Unwin.

Dworkin, Ronald (1985): 'Why Liberals Should Care About Equality', in R. Dworkin, *A Matter of Principle*, Cambridge, MA: Harvard University Press.

Feinberg, W. (1989): 'Foundationalism and Recent Critiques of Education', *Educational Theory*, Vol. 39, No. 2, pp. 133-38.

Friedman, Milton (1955): 'The Role of Government in Education', in Robert Solo (ed.), *Economics and the Public Interest*, New Brunswick: Rutgers University Press.

Friedman, Milton (1962): *Capitalism and Freedom*, Chicago: University of Chicago Press.

Habakkuk, H.J. (1962): *American and British Technology in the Nineteenth Century*, Cambridge: Cambridge University Press.

Hague, D. (1991): *Beyond Universities: A New Republic of the Intellect*, Hobart Paper 115, London: The Institute of Economic Affairs.

Institute for Employment Studies (1996): *What Do Graduates Really Do?*, Falmer: Institute for Employment Studies.

Kerr, C. (1972): *The Use of the University*, Cambridge, MA: Harvard University Press.

Le Grand, Julian (1987): 'The Middle-Class Use of the British Social Services', in R. E. Goodin and Julian Le Grand, *Not Only the Poor: The Middle Classes and the Welfare State,* London: Allen and Unwin.

MacIntyre, Alasdair (1990): *Three Rival Versions of Moral Enquiry*, London: Duckworth.

Mendus, Susan (1992): 'All the King's Horses and All the King's Men: justifying higher education', *Journal of Philosophy of Education*, Vol. 26, No. 2, pp. 173-82.

Murphy, James (1991): 'Over-educated and Under-employed: British Graduates in the 1990s', *Journal of Education Policy*, Vol. 6, No. 2, pp. 239-44.

National Committee of Inquiry into Higher Education (NCIHE) (1997): *Higher Education in the Learning Society*, London: HMSO.

Organisation for Economic Co-operation and Development (OECD) (1996): *Education at a Glance: Education Indicators*, Paris: OECD.

Peacock, Alan T., and Wiseman, Jack (1964): *Education for Democrats,* Hobart Paper 25, London: Institute of Economic Affairs.

Rawls, John (1972): *A Theory of Justice*, Oxford: Clarendon Press.

Sanderson, M. (1972): *The Universities and British Industry 1850-1970*, London: Routledge and Kegan Paul.

Shattock, Michael (1994): *The UGC and the Management of British Universities*, Buckingham: Society for Research into Higher Education & Open University Press.

Sperling, John, and Tucker, Robert W. (1997): *For-Profit Higher Education: developing a world-class workforce*, New Brunswick and London: Transaction Publishers.

Tooley, James (1995a): *Disestablishing the School*, Aldershot: Avebury.

Tooley, James (1995b): 'Putting the Political Back into Autonomy', in W. Kohli (ed.), *Critical Conversations in Philosophy of Education*, New York: Routledge.

Tooley, James (1996): *Education without the State*, London: Institute of Economic Affairs.

Tooley, James (1997): 'Choice and Diversity in Education: A Defence', *Oxford Review of Education*, Vol. 23, No. 1, pp. 103-16.

West, E.G. (1970): *Education and the State*, London: Institute of Economic Affairs.

West, Edwin G. (1995): 'The Economics of Higher Education', in John W. Sommer (ed.), *The Academy in Crisis: the political economy of higher education*, Oakland, CA: The Independent Institute.

The Radical Implications of Modularity

Adrian Seville, City University

1 | Introduction

There is considerable agreement in Universities in the UK that a method of delivery of teaching conveniently labelled 'modularity' is an appropriate way forward in developing a flexible system of 'mass' higher education, in which perhaps 33 per cent, according to government targets, or even 40 per cent, according to the CBI recommendation, of the young adult population will be involved by the turn of the century. The final report of the Committee of Enquiry into the Review of the Academic Year, the 'Flowers' Report, summarised the position as follows:

> There is a widespread intention to introduce modular courses, where they have not been introduced already, and there is a general consensus that a module should optimally be about 15 taught weeks (including assessment) (HEFCE, 1993, p. 5).

The Flowers Report is concerned only with practicalities such as facilitating timetabling by the uniformity of convenient teaching blocks and increasing the flexibility of the teaching year. For it, the label 'module' evidently means no more than the sub-division and packaging of higher education courses into self-contained units. This, however, is a 'weak' description of modularity. At the other end of the spectrum there lies a form which – this paper argues – heralds a radical 'type change' for higher education in England.

In this 'strong' form of modularity, modules are made available in a highly flexible way, to students who, by informed choice of these modules, take responsibility for shaping their own education. Successful completion of a module results in the gaining of a corresponding 'credit', expressed as a defined number of credit points associated with the module. By credit accumulation and, where appropriate, credit accumulation transfer (CAT) – not necessarily restricted to academic institutions, still less to single institutions – these students may achieve recognised qualifications having wide currency, such as diplomas, first degrees, and higher degrees.

This transfer of the responsibility of choice brings about radical change. It opens genuine and exciting new channels for student 'empowerment', and will lead to institutions of higher education becoming more responsive to the needs and requirements of the newly empowered 'consumers' of education. However, it also necessitates a fundamental reappraisal of what is meant by quality in education, of its funding mechanisms and of its ultimate planning and direction. These are the concerns which this paper aims to address.

The debate on these issues in the UK has been remarkable both for its lack of focus and its lack of intensity. The wide majority acceptance of modularity as an organising principle, or administrative convenience, particularly in the context of the Flowers Report, has set the tone for discussion. Evidently, the advocates of 'strong' modularity have been content to let the main issues of principle lie dormant until the organisational pressures have taken effect.

However, the Robertson report (HEQC, 1994) commissioned by the Higher Education Quality Council (HEQC) proposed an over-arching credit accumulation scheme, based upon modularity, to cover all higher and further education. Its advocacy of student empowerment has begun to raise sensitivities, especially in the 'old' universities, to the nature of the changes implied. Robertson clearly recognises the issues:

> Some informed opinion in universities remains suspicious of the introduction of credit systems and modularity. Their concerns go beyond a superficial antipathy to markets or a collectivist opposition to the individualisation of the curriculum in higher education. They believe that what is at stake is the place and purpose of the University in the modern world. Is it to retain its principal purpose as a centre of intellectual rationality, coherence and moral integrity? Or is it to join other organisations of the 'post-modern' world in intellectual fragmentation, 'consumerist' superficiality and moral relativism? (HEQC, 1994, p. 332)

Response to the report (HEQC, 1995, p. 4) shows a profound division of opinion between two groups: on the one hand, a majority of universities, specialist colleges and professional (particularly statutory) bodies; on the other, a minority of universities, some professional (non-statutory) bodies and some employers' organisations.

Both groups demonstrate a concern for issues such as quality and standards in credit-based learning. Nevertheless, the difference in emphasis between them is wide. To the first group, credit-based learning is a useful institutional mechanism to facilitate, for example, modularity and the transfer of students between institutions where appropriate. To the second group, the report's approach promises the emergence of a single unitary national credit framework applicable to institutions and the world of work/employment, one which will organise all post-school education including higher education.

The conclusion reached by the HEQC is that it should concentrate on the quality assurance of credit-based systems, by supporting institutions' efforts to ensure that new structures for delivering teaching and learning are subject to the same critical review as more traditional or conventional ones (HEQC, 1995, p. v). However, the HEQC recognises that the development of credit frameworks raises issues about the definitions and assurance of academic standards 'in perhaps their most acute form', although these wider issues are not directly addressed.

This paper is a contribution to this important debate. Its purpose is not to engage in a hand-to-hand fight against the spread of modularity. For the author believes that modularity in higher education is here to stay – it is a useful and adaptable mechanism which, like any powerful mechanism, needs to be handled well. The paper aims to expose the frailty of the theoretical and practical framework of higher education on which modularity is now being so extensively hung, and to make some suggestions for how it might be strengthened. If this difficult work is not undertaken, there is a danger that the proper – and valuable – development of modularity in higher education will be threatened by an understandable backlash.

The depth of the problem turns out to be considerable. For example, the differences between the opposing positions cannot be understood or resolved without examining the question: 'What is the fundamental nature of a degree?' Indeed, it will be argued in this paper that the form of the question is flawed, in that it assumes that there is an answer. The preferred approach is to recognise and, if possible, label and quantify the diversity that is now deeply rooted in the educational systems of the UK.

Although this paper was written before the publication of Sir Ron Dearing's review of higher education, its thrust – that radical changes in the structure of higher education are inevitable – recognises the forces which led to the setting up of the review body, and will usefully sit alongside the public deliberations of the outcomes of that review.

The paper begins by setting out the characteristics of 'traditional' higher education and comparing these with modular schemes (Chapter 2). It then briefly reviews some of the distortions in the higher education market, before moving on to one of the key issues of the debate: can quality in higher education be maintained if the system moves towards modularisation? (Chapter 3). This in itself raises the troubling issue of how quality is to be maintained now, and suggests that the current mechanisms are not entirely satisfactory. Chapter 4 then explores higher education funding mechanisms, and how alternatives may be put into place to facilitate effective modularisation. Finally, Chapter 5 points to the future possibilities of higher education in the light of this discussion.

2 | Modular and Traditional Schemes

Characteristics of Traditional Higher Education: the Cohort Scheme

The key concept in understanding what we may call 'traditional' higher education, higher education before the introduction of modularisation, is that of the *cohort*: the well-defined student group which undertakes a *course*. Figure 1 indicates in a schematic way the educational process by which the cohort passes from a region of states of knowledge and capability A to region B, each line indicating the progress of a particular student. Some student lines terminate – by drop-out or failure – before region B is reached. One or two (not shown) may diverge from the main envelope, for example by acquiring knowledge or capability well beyond the expected norm. But the aim is to bring most of the cohort to the region B, which corresponds to the standard of the degree or other qualification.

This is obviously a simplified model: the reality would, for example, require many dimensions fully to show knowledge and capability. Yet it already includes some interesting characteristics. The model implies some continuity of interaction, so that 'progress' is observable. It also implies some uniformity of starting states and of the tuition process. From these derive notions of 'fairness': everyone starts more or less the same, everyone is treated the same, so that achievement is on merit. There is a 'pastoral' role: those who stray are brought back to the educational 'track'. The direction is clearly marked out and the timescale for completion is ordained.

It makes sense to talk about the progress of the group and to standardise achievement using the statistics of the group, taking into account continuity with groups from previous years. Admission standards are important in achieving reasonable – though not total – group homogeneity: the traditional course can benefit greatly from diversity in student profile within the cohort group, whether diversity of age, experience or culture. This is a model typified by strong formation of the student and strong identity with the institution. Here, 'formation' is used in the sense familiar in professions such as Engineering, to mean the shaping of the student by education and experience.

Characteristics of Higher Education in the Modular Scheme

In higher education based on a student-led modular scheme, education loses the assumptions set out in the previous section. Many, perhaps most, modularisation programmes presently in place do not yet have the 'full freedoms' of this idealised model. However, throughout the text we use the terms *modular scheme* and *module-based* to refer to a 'fully-evolved' modular programme, with significant transfer of power to the student, rather than to the use of modularisation merely as an administrative device within what remains essentially a traditional, service-based, institution.

There is no assumption of uniformity of starting states, no continuity of observation and interaction, hence no observable path and no uniformity of process – though the individual processes may be highly monitored through centralised record systems. There are only individual 'learning transitions' and even these may or may not be brought about by experiences within the institution: the individual becomes a 'consumer' of various educational commodities, variously available in a 'market'. This is a model typified by strong individualisation and weak socialisation.

The distinction is shown in Figure 2. Now, all that can be seen are the labels of individual students 1, 2 etc., in states A initially and, at some later time, in states B. Some of these students have achieved states within the 'qualification space', some not. There is no defined course, no timescale, and intermediate progress is not necessarily defined. The difficulty in standardising assessments in the absence of a well-defined cohort is considerable. Indeed, some students may exceed the exit standards in some areas even on entry. The emphasis therefore tends to be on 'learning outcomes', meaning specifications of the knowledge and competencies which a person awarded the qualification would be expected to have, rather than on the standard expected of a cohort group taught in a particular way. This is a crucial difference of emphasis, which will be explored fully below.

Figure 1: The Cohort Scheme

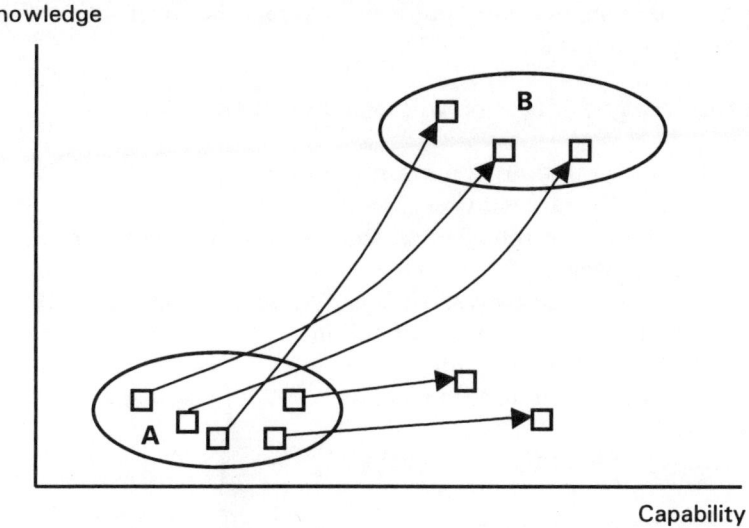

Figure 2: The Modular Scheme

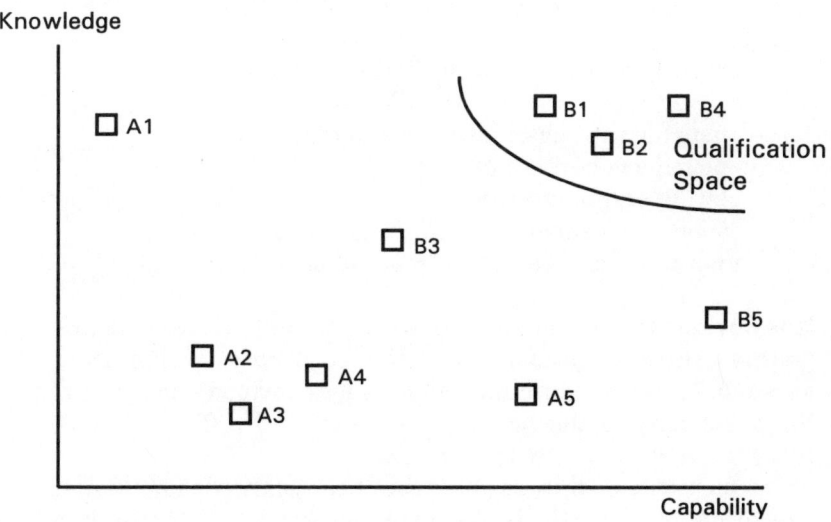

Provision of Modular Higher Education

The modular model has implications for the provision of education, as follows:

The *marketing* of education will need to include:

- the determination of market requirements;
- design of modules to specification;
- specifying the interfacing, that is, how modules join on to each other;
- specifying pathways, that is, what modules may be joined to make up a qualification;
- packaging and labelling;
- advertising and information.

The *delivery* of education will include:

- availability of modules (where, when, how);
- cost effectiveness of provision;
- budgets and planning;
- resource management, including human resources.

The *quality control* of education will include:

- devising and maintaining 'industry' standards;
- convergence on these standards;
- ensuring interchangeability and currency;
- ensuring coherence of pathways;
- testing and monitoring;
- consumer feedback;
- upgrading and re-development of modules.

It is obvious to anyone familiar with planning, marketing and quality control in industry that this constitutes a significant and demanding programme. What is less obvious – because of the familiarity of the headings – is just how difficult it is to carry it out successfully in education.

In particular, this is because the 'market' for higher education in the UK is, as explored below, distorted and under-informed. Delivery of higher education is still substantially provider-oriented. As far as quality control is concerned, some of the tools for the job do not exist. All this means that the smooth provision of modular higher education faces obstacles both in theory and in practice.

Organisation of the Modular Scheme

The typical organisation of a modular degree scheme (Watson, 1989) on the principles outlined above can be deduced: within a given institution, there will be modules of various kinds (not just lecture courses) and at various levels. Modules will be provided by 'departments' which contain the relevant subject specialists. Students will enrol upon 'programmes' which make use of modules, often from more than one department. (This scheme can usefully be thought of as a matrix, with the departments as columns and the programme areas as rows). Programme co-ordinators are designated to have responsibility for the academic coherence of each programme area. The heads of department have responsibility for the provision of the modules. Staff having overall responsibility for the management of the modular scheme are also designated. There is negotiation, within an internal market structure, between the programme co-ordinators – who are agents for the students as ultimate consumers – and the departmental providers, working within the overall management plans and constraints. At the level of the individual student, the pastoral role becomes subsumed in 'consumer advice' (guidance), with any tutorial support being provided within each module. However, the need for individual tutorial support is less than in the 'traditional' model because there is less need to keep a student on the normal progression track. A student who has difficulty with a module may drop out, choose a different module or come back later.

The modular scheme is designed to be well adapted to credit accumulation and transfer (CAT), with recognition of prior learning, including prior experiential learning. This is because modules can be well-specified in terms of prior requirements and learning outcomes. Similarly, individual student programmes can include modules derived outside the institution, including learning at the place of work, in other institutions, or by distance learning, including particularly the Open University.

Despite this clear specification, cleanly-running systems have proved difficult to devise and operate. A conference held at the University of Central Lancashire, for example, had the evocative title: 'Avoiding the Chaos of Credit Accumulation and Transfer'. There are indeed some fundamental weaknesses in the modularity concept which, if not addressed, will tend to lead to inchoate systems.

Semesterisation

The central importance of the module in the organisational structure means that extra-modular activity is inconvenient. There is thus pressure, for example, to contain examination and assessment wholly within the module, though some schemes employ 'synoptic' modules to give an overview.

Modules of a year's duration are regarded as inflexible, and especially difficult for part-time study modes. The traditional 10-week term, on the other hand, is inconveniently short, if assessment is to be comprised within it. There is thus a tendency to regard a 15-week semester as a good compromise, representing half a traditional academic year. The possibility of offering three such semesters in the calendar year is an added attraction, representing greater (although arguably not maximal) use of physical plant. Where this is done, most students attend two semesters, though the possibility of intensive courses – for example, six semesters in two calendar years – is not ruled out, especially for mature students (the example of the two-year degrees at the University of Buckingham is relevant here).

Likewise, most staff will teach on only two semesters each year, though it is notable that universities with little research funding are finding it difficult to get an economic teaching-only output from their staff without violating this condition.

Pressures for Modularisation: Diversity of Student Intake

The main driving force in the educational 'market' that favours 'strong' modularity as against the 'traditional' system is the increasing diversity of the student intake. This growing diversity arises from:

- the advent of 'access' courses and BTEC as a significant alternative to the 'A' level entry qualification, with National Vocational Qualification (NVQ and especially

General National Vocational Qualification [GNVQ]) routes likely to continue the trend;

- the flight away from Mathematics and Physics A-levels, which means that diversity of intake is especially marked in subjects such as Engineering;

- the decrease in homogeneity of school sixth forms, both in the private and the public sectors;

- the increasing importance of Further Education institutions in mediating entry to Higher Education, both by franchised or validated courses and by transfer of students to Higher Education Institutions, facilitated by CAT schemes;

- the significant change in the age pattern of entry as the numbers of students in Higher Education increase;

- the likelihood of increased European Union student numbers;

- the substantial numbers of overseas students already in the system.

It is, of course, possible to overstate the consequences of this diversity. University courses – even when based firmly on A-level entry – have always had to cope with the diversity of A-level syllabuses, which have lacked agreed cores, and with the diversity of teaching and learning choices accompanying them. It is therefore likely that, apart possibly from a few highly-selective institutions, all institutions of higher education will need increasingly to find means of adapting teaching and learning requirements to accommodate the diversity of their student mix. Accordingly, there will be almost universal pressure to move towards flexible modular schemes. Allied to this is the political pressure, not exclusively from the left, to open up higher education, making it less 'élitist', and at the same time to make higher education cheaper for the state by encouraging part-time, distance or work-based modes of study.

Strengths and Weaknesses of the Modular Scheme

The main strength of the modular scheme of higher education is that it is well adapted to absorbing a number of pressures on higher education. These include the need to accommodate the diversity of student numbers, as mentioned above. Other pressures to which it can respond include:

- The modular scheme, which allows students to retake modules in a flexible way, or to substitute other modules for those not passed, provides weaker students with evidence of what they have achieved, softening the edges of failure by substituting a modified success.

- The need for economy of provision; as resource per student falls during the expansion of higher education towards mass participation, the pressure is on to maximise class size by use of standardised modules. Small-group tuition is not a usual feature of the modular scheme and this also cuts costs, though the need for individual counselling on module choice to some extent offsets the savings.

- Individual choice and individual control of learning are, in principle, attractive to students.

- Competition arises because of the availability of many learning modes, not all of them institutionally based. Institutions need therefore to be able to give credit for prior learning and experience and to accommodate students who wish to combine different modes, at different stages.

- Specialisation of institutions is favoured, since it is impossible for a single institution to meet all learning requirements. This implies that the modules provided by an institution should have currency in other institutions.

- Accountability and quality control is felt to be achievable within a scheme of standardisation and specification of modules more easily than through the ill-defined in-built standards associated with traditional learning.

These are the strengths of the system. However, modular-based higher education has a number of intrinsic weaknesses as compared with the traditional model. Examples are:

- The reduced control by institutions over students' learning strategies.

- Increased possibility of fraud, especially in non-institutional learning, where the extent that the student is 'helped' by work colleagues is difficult to monitor.

- Difficulty in monitoring teaching quality, since progress of a group is no longer a meaningful concept.

Controls for these can, however, be built in, for example by using various forms of invigilated continuous assessment, with feedback to the student, or use of oral examinations. It is also true that in some traditional schemes the extent of non-invigilated coursework leads to questions about standards: buying an essay is not unknown even in the most august educational establishments.

The problem of monitoring teaching quality is a separate one. Direct observation of teaching delivery has come late to British universities but obviously becomes crucial in the case of education which is not cohort-based. A more fundamental weakness is that certain features normally (or ideally) associated with traditional cohort-based education are absent:

- The requirement to absorb, analyse and interpret material under pressures of time and intensity.

- The requirement for some social adaptation to the institution: this may matter less for mature students who come from the workplace and are already capable of interacting well with their colleagues; but for many students straight from school the 'humanising' effects of the university as a social institution mean much to future success and happiness.

- The opportunity to derive intellectual stimulus from interaction with the cohort group, engaged in the same or similar study, so that high standards are encouraged by example and so that weaker students can be helped along.

- The sense of cohort identity for the student, possibly leading to more general psychological difficulties, and also perhaps leading to a loss in staff involvement with an identifiable cohort.

- The possibility of clear-cut failure may be virtually excluded by the general availability of other modules to attempt and other modes of study: this may mean that public funds are misused to continue support for a student who has turned out to be unsuited to degree-level work.

- The advantages of modular flexibility do not translate easily into 'linear' subjects such as Mathematics, whereas building on a firm shared foundation from year to year is a strong feature of cohort-based education in these subjects.

Finally, there are the administrative difficulties:

- Credit-based systems require good information management, with a corresponding requirement for resources of equipment and trained staff.

- The administrative systems need to be able to interface with the student in a way which fully recognises the student's responsibility for his or her learning strategy.

- Such high levels of student responsibility need to be developed, not taken for granted.

- The administration of a complex modular scheme will tend to interact/interfere more with academic staff than is usual under a traditional scheme.

- The increased centralisation of administration normal in a modular scheme can produce sensations of remoteness for the academic staff, as compared with department or school-based systems.

The discussion above has been based substantially on a comparison with traditional cohort-based education. However, it has to be admitted that this does not always deliver all the virtues implied by that comparison. In particular, the analysis of the student experience below indicates that there are serious causes for concern about what is now being offered to students who are following traditional programmes. Too often, what should be the systematic learning development of a student through carefully planned and delivered teaching becomes instead a distressing saga of missed lectures and tutorials, with a desperate chase at the end of the year to make up for lost opportunities.

It should also be evident from the tone of the language used to express the different viewpoints that there is a lack of shared criteria against which to evaluate 'strengths' and 'weaknesses'. This is one aspect of the fundamental lack of clarity as to the nature of a degree, to be explored further below. Nevertheless, it is clear that the positive and negative features of modular schemes have the potential to affect several dimensions of the educational process:

- the quality of the output;
- the student experience;
- the cost per graduate;
- the staff experience;
- the diversity and flexibility of provision.

All of these dimensions will be addressed in what follows, so that suggestions on policy may be advanced.

Distortions of the Market in Higher Education

It may be argued by some that the market could simply respond to the consumer pressures outlined above, and provide modularisation if this is what is demanded. However, the current 'market' in higher education is substantially distorted, compared with a conventional market in which suppliers would compete on quality, price, service and diversity of provision. One obvious distortion is the fact that the state pays a 'subsidy' towards the cost of higher education. This is not addressed in this paper, on the grounds that I believe it is not realistic for a developed nation to spend nothing in support of higher education – though it is not argued that the existing funding, still less its distribution, is necessarily optimal.[1] Other distortions include:

- The nature of a given qualification (an honours degree, say) is held to be uniform across the system, so that institutions do not compete overtly on output quality.

---

[1] A critique of this key assumption is found in James Tooley's Critical Introduction to this paper.

- The cost per graduate is being driven by the Government's funding model towards the system average, which is itself declining in real terms. Institutions are not being encouraged to compete on price. Furthermore, they are operating a system-wide institutional veto on charging additional tuition fees for undergraduate courses (though not for postgraduate courses).

- The student experience is constrained by peculiarities of student support funding, whereby full-time students have the benefit of Mandatory Award funding, whereas part-time students do not.

- The experience of academic staff is substantially determined by the opportunities for research, as the demands on teaching time grow uniformly heavier across the system; research opportunities are themselves determined largely by the Research Assessment Exercises operated by the Funding Councils.

- The illogicalities of the difference in treatment of full-time and part-time students mean that the market is segmented; there are considerable rigidities arising from outside constraints (such as the timetable of the A-level system) which make alternative patterns of education difficult; and there are historic prejudices for and against certain patterns.

Furthermore, the market is characterised by imperfect information on the part of the students, viewed as customers. In the USA, information is much more readily available to both potential applicants, graduates and employers. For example, the student transcript is a universal document, detailing success and failure over time in a way that our degree classification does not begin to approach. Again, the employment placement record of leavers from MBA courses is made available as part of marketing. Overlying all this, the 'image' of each different institution is carefully polished and there are substantial industries devoted to producing information and comparisons in summary form, both as hard copy and on IT networks. The UK has not advanced far down this road.

Given this background, we now turn to explore the

fundamental issues of the problems of quality control in modularised higher education (Chapter 3).

3 | Quality

Recent discussion of how to ensure quality control in the context of modularisation has raised the exceedingly important question of how current quality control procedures work for existing, traditional degree courses. In this chapter, we point to the numerous and troubling difficulties with the current quality control régime in higher education in the UK. We also point out the complexities which would be necessary for any centrally-planned solution to these problems. We leave it to the reader to decide if these complexities could be surmounted, or whether a more radical solution to the problem of quality control in higher education is necessary.

Quality Control in Higher Education

The 'quality' of the degree award is a key aspect of its nature. In England, the government has instituted a quality control régime, purportedly to safeguard employers and home and overseas student applicants alike. The argument goes something like this: there are too many degree-awarding institutions for employers and students to be able to judge each on its merits – in round figures, even at first degree level, there are about 200 institutions each offering around 100 courses, not counting the bewildering variety of modular combinations. Both employers and students, however, can be safeguarded by the national system of quality control. Moreover, the quality of the British degree is regarded as a key asset in the attraction of overseas students. Their fees now constitute an important resource for many institutions. They – or the authorities of their countries of origin – likewise cannot be expected to look closely at the different courses provided. Nevertheless, all will be safeguarded by the government's quality control systems. The reality, however, is different, as explained below.

Responsibility for quality control in higher education in England is divided as follows:

- The Higher Education Quality Council (HEQC) ('owned' by the institutions) audits institutions with regard to the effectiveness, completeness and operation of their procedures.

- The Higher Education Funding Council for England (HEFCE) ('owned' by the Department for Education and Employment) assesses delivery of teaching and learning on a subject-by-subject basis across all institutions; there is no direct relationship between quality and funding, though the rare cases of unsatisfactory quality would, if unrectified, eventually lead to a partial withdrawal of funding.

- Separately, the HEFCE periodically assesses the research performance of institutions for quality and volume, with a formula thereafter to calculate funding mechanically.

- Each degree-awarding institution is responsible for its own academic standards, mediated by a system of external examiners, which is itself under national review (Silver, Stennett and Williams, 1995); many such institutions validate other (non-university) institutions which provide courses leading to degrees.

- Many professions accredit specified degree courses for the purposes of exempting graduates wholly or partially from professional examinations.

It is not surprising that this complex system – with doubtful routes for overall accountability – has allowed unanswered questions to arise, in respect not only of modular schemes, but raised particularly by them.

In all this supposedly-impressive battery of quality-control mechanisms, *the only one directly and universally* concerned with the maintenance of output standards is that of the external examiners, though the professional bodies have a similar (but more limited) role to play in respect of the courses which they accredit. Crucially, a recent report (Silver, Stennett & Williams, 1995) expresses growing concern about how the external examiner system now operates, against the background of increased student numbers, the widespread introduction of modular programmes, new patterns of assessing students and new institutional and national quality assessment and assurance procedures.

By contrast, the assessment of teaching by the HEFCE is directed principally to determining whether or not the institution is meeting its own institutionally-set objectives. This recognises the diversity amongst institutions but does nothing directly to ensure that the supposedly-uniform output standards are being met. Statements by Ministers from the previous Conservative Government ('a degree is a degree') are intended to warn against this relativism.

The Government and the Higher Education Institutions now argue that a single system of academic quality assurance is necessary, bringing together audit and assessment; it is necessary also to articulate this with professional accreditation. However, in this chapter it will be pointed out how inordinately complicated such a system would have to be: it is not clear that such a system (which inevitably has to start from the current diversity of practice and aims) will have the ability to do more than recognise a corresponding diversity of standards. If the challenge which this presents is not (or cannot be) met, demands may well emerge for a different approach to quality control altogether – one relying on more authentic market mechanisms.

This chapter highlights the difficulties with the current system, and with any likely alternative.

Relativism in Standards

'Relativism' in standards was for long a hidden issue in British higher education. When the (now superseded) Council for National Academic Awards (CNAA) was set up to validate the degree-level teaching of the then polytechnics, the brief expressed in the CNAA's original Charter was to ensure comparability of standards with those of the ('old') university sector. A cynic might, with some justification, say that the CNAA was more successful at reproducing, and enforcing on the polytechnics, the bureaucratic procedures of the unreconstructed 'old' university system than in ensuring, in any testable way, comparability of outputs. This, though, would be to neglect the good work done by the CNAA in systematising the approach to evaluation of course proposals, making good use of external advisers.

In any case, the commitment to comparability was removed

when the CNAA Charter was revised, so that the polytechnic sector became free-standing in this regard. Next, many of the polytechnics became essentially self-validating, under agreements with the CNAA. Finally, the demise of the CNAA occurred, with all polytechnics becoming self-validating and being granted university status under the final abolition of the 'binary' system of higher education. The sensitivities existing were such that to talk of possible differences in standard was to risk being labelled as opposing this (entirely necessary) development.

The purpose of this discussion is not to argue that 'old' universities all have (or have had) higher output standards than 'new': there are too many counter-examples to allow any such generalisation. Indeed, if the definition of quality is widened from that narrow ground of academic achievement which is the traditional home of the British honours degree, it may be argued that some of the ex-polytechnics have exceeded the old universities in areas such as enterprise, communications, team-work, industry-based learning and projects which are of high relevance to employment. The intention instead is to emphasise that – though lip-service may have been paid to the uniformity of standard of a British degree – there has in fact been no system in place which would justify confidence in any such uniformity. Nor, more fundamentally, is there any agreement on how such standards would be determined, measured and applied.

What is a Degree?

This leads us to the question of what exactly is a degree? To reply to this question that 'a degree is a degree' suggests that, even if a degree cannot be defined, the informed observer would recognise one if it came into view. It recalls, to no good effect, the early attempts of the HEFCE to define teaching quality for its assessors: 'Quality is difficult to define but you will know it if you see it.'

The approach will not do for us here, because modularity – especially in its strong form – makes some degrees unrecognisable by any conventional profiles. An alternative approach is to ask: what may a degree be used operationally to signify? The list below is illustrative of categories rather than exhaustive of function:

- to indicate that a single academic subject has been pursued to some depth;

- to indicate that several or many subjects have been pursued to a lesser depth;

- to signify practical competence in some area;

- to obtain whole or partial exemption from the requirements (statutory or not) of a particular profession, vocation or employment;

- to mark that study has been pursued at a particular educational institution (with a high or low reputation – generally or in a particular subject area);

- to mark that (some) study, although the outcome is validated by an educational institution, has occurred elsewhere (for instance, in industry or abroad);

- to imply that the person concerned is capable of (some of):

- concentrated and rapid study
- independent study
- research
- persistence
- team work
- problem solving
- effective communication in speech/writing, etc.
- effective use of information systems
- effective use of computer systems

- to suggest that the person concerned may have acquired some benefits, not usually assessed, connected with:

- general social skills
- networks and contacts for the future
- self-confidence
- independence of mind
- growing up
- physical development
- moral development
- broadening of interests.

This raises the further question of whether all modes of learning and examination for a degree would be equally satisfactory to different employers. For example, some employers – such as the top accountancy firms – will take a good degree result as signifying the ability to learn new skills under pressure. Obviously, they are unlikely to be satisfied by a student who has obtained a good classification only after many re-tries over a long period. However, other employers, less concerned with potential for learning new high-level material, will be impressed by the qualities of perseverance shown by this student.[1]

This is not just a question about the academic record of a student. That would be easy to deal with since an official transcript of a graduate's progress to the degree could in future be prepared through the new centralised student record system (the Higher Education Statistics Agency, HESA), even if several different institutions had been involved over different periods of time.

In fact, the question lies at the heart of designing the degree curriculum and the examination process. If there is no agreement as to the purpose of a degree or what it signifies, standardisation becomes logically impossible.

If the above attempt to operationalise the degree is too complicated, how might it be improved? It is evident that all these aspects of a degree would occupy many different factorial axes in any operational specification. A separation might be tried along the lines:

- academic standards reached (breadth and depth);

- professional/vocational accreditation;

- study skills acquired;

- employment-related skills (communication and interpersonal skills especially);

---

[1] It is interesting that the 'modular A levels' which are being developed alongside traditional A levels are giving rise to similar concerns (*The Times*, 28 December 1994). For example, some advocates of modularity believe that failure rates can appropriately be reduced to near-zero by allowing re-tries as necessary to achieve a pass, under conditions of continuous assessment.

- potential for further study or research.

Even though such a list merely shows how incomplete such a separation would be – a very rough bundling of 'threads' into 'strands' – it does enable the question to be posed operationally: how many and which of these strands is a degree supposed to certify?

It is evident that even for conventional degrees at traditional institutions the certification is incomplete and varies considerably (for example, between disciplines). For modular schemes, and non-traditional institutions, the variety is endless.

Measurement of Success

A further question is raised: on what basis should a degree be classified? Classification of honours degrees is not universal in the world but is regarded as an important feature of the British system, useful in motivating students and useful in providing employers with a handy guide to the 'quality' of an applicant.

There are two fundamentally-opposed objective means of measuring success, differentiated by the educational jargon terms of 'norm referencing' and 'learning outcomes'. Additionally, there is a measurement technique, usually (and misleadingly) called 'using absolute standards'.

'Norm referencing' means that the performance of an individual is judged relative to his or her cohort, or to a series of cohorts standardised over time. In its simplest form, it would mean that (for example) the pass rate is predetermined and the nominal pass mark is adjusted (moderated, standardised) to achieve this result. For example, when the A-level was first established in 1951, there was a pre-ordained failure rate of 30 per cent and a system of fixed percentages in the various pass bands was used up to 1975. This consistency of outcome enables accurate standardisation of questions in both setting and marking.

The A-level boards have used this kind of standardisation to move away from strict norm-referencing and now grade according to performance on standardised questions. Although it is a grading process which is capable of considerable statistical justification and refinement, cultural, curricular and other secular changes make it difficult to insist upon any absolute uniformity of standards – and this form of secular drift has been the subject of considerable criticism in the media recently. However, where cohorts are large and reasonably homogeneous, the procedures used by the A-level boards do give results of considerable reliability within a subject, though inter-subject comparisons are less reliable. Indeed, much of the supposed 'grade drift' of recent years can be ascribed to changes in the subject mix encompassed within the average of all candidates.

Universities are traditionally supposed to use norm referencing but usually they do so without the same statistical refinement as is applied by the A-level boards. For one thing, the university cohorts are smaller. Questions are imperfectly standardised and marking is also more judgemental and subjective. The result is that marks are not always statistically standardised, though they are usually moderated in some way. Students are thus judged against the standards of individual examiners as well as relative to the performance of the cohort as a whole.

This collective feeling for standards in their own discipline is highly important to the academic staff of a university and any attempt by management to interfere with it is resented as anti-professional. This 'internal' set of standards is of prime importance – the external examiner can have some influence on the results at the margins but, if the internal standards are inadequate or compromised, correction from outside is virtually impossible.

These internal standards – with all their evident subjectivity – are often referred to as 'absolute standards'. They can of course be documented, to assist in their transmission and to enhance the air of permanence. But at their heart remains the element of academic judgement. It is likely that, with practice, academic staff could extend their judgement of standards – built up through years of familiarity with the development of students on traditional courses – to fully-modular student-centred schemes. However, certain caveats arise:

- that the measurement is essentially comparative and needs (at present) to be based on experience of a reasonably traditional course;

- the overall result is an amalgam of the views of individual examiners, with no universal agreement on how the views should be combined operationally;

- the standards are not transparent and are not obviously portable to another institution or to another subject area.

Nonetheless, these judgements of standards are all we have to define and protect the degree standard in this country and they should not be decried because of the difficulty in making them explicit.

The 'Learning Outcomes' Debate

Against this background – and in part as a reaction against the academic 'establishment' which is an evident necessity for maintaining the 'absolute' but internal standards discussed above – it is not surprising that an attempt has been made to achieve external transparency and portability of standards. That attempt is the radical approach of determining the 'learning outcomes' which the individual has achieved. The bundle of positive learning outcomes required for each particular level of qualification in a subject is specified, area by area, in documented and published form.

The argument is seductive. It cuts across all the arcane discussion of standards applying within an educational institution. If, for example, a prospective employer wants to know whether an applicant has proved capable of performing some task, all that is necessary is to consult the manual of the qualification presented: if the task is listed as a positive learning outcome, the necessary assurance is given.

This is the fundamental approach adopted by those responsible for the GNVQ (General National Vocational Qualification) system. The key point here is that judging an individual by a learning outcome – something specific (but not necessarily easy), such as the ability to wire an electrical component correctly or detect a complicated fault – is well suited to lower-level vocational qualifications, where competency in achieving a representative bundle of tasks is what is sought. However, the approach is less obviously suited to degree work: for example, understanding partial differential equations, where there are many levels of 'understanding', requiring knowledge of concepts rather than straightforward performance of tasks. This question cannot be ducked, since the National Vocational Qualification (NVQ) system is intended to reach up to and include degree level qualifications.

The difficulty is recognised in a recent consultative paper, which, because of its importance, is worth quoting at length:

> Knowledge is an integral part of competence at all levels of occupation and, in NVQs...it must be demonstrable through assessment. At lower levels much of it can be inferred in the process of assessment; at higher levels of occupation however, mastery and exploitation of bodies and patterns of knowledge, of concepts and paradigms, of precedent and process is vital for satisfactory performance. Similarly, while ethical issues and value judgements are encountered at all levels in the workplace, the nature of work at higher levels places a new and vital importance on the need for standards in these areas to be incorporated within higher level vocational qualifications.
>
> The development of higher level vocational qualifications therefore demands a different model of knowledge and values in educational competence. Higher Education, Statutory and Professional Bodies will play a vital role in this work, helping to guarantee that such qualifications are at the leading edge of occupational practice. ...
>
> The development of higher level vocational qualifications will require further work to explore approaches to assessment which are capable of capturing the complexities of occupational roles at this level, for example high levels of personal responsibility, unpredictable nature of problems and capacity for self improvement and evaluation. These must be achieved using approaches which are sufficiently robust, demanding and cost effective to earn public support. (Employment Department, 1995).

Previously, there has been a tendency to over-simplify the issues. Advocates of vocational qualifications have tended to assume that their current methodologies can be extended without fundamental change to degree level qualifications. The new document sets out an agenda for discussion that is very welcome. However, there is an assumption that a unifying framework can be agreed, with good assessment procedures commanding respect across the academic community as well as in the world of employment and the professions. It is a tall order, given the background set out above: the fundamentals that would need to be addressed run very deep.

Disturbing Conclusions on Quality

The conclusions from the foregoing sections are disturbing:

- The quality control system at national level is fragmented and under review.

- The external examiner system is proving incapable of bearing the weight imposed upon it by changes such as the expansion of student numbers and the increase in modular courses, and is itself also under review.

- Relativism of degree standards is being openly recognised, exposing differences between subjects and between groups of institutions.

- There is no agreement on whether the award of a particular qualification signifies potential or achievement.

- The standards of universities (though real) are neither portable nor transparent.

- Specification of learning outcomes, as presently developed, is not a suitable method for setting standards in higher education.

These conclusions are the more disturbing since the personal remedies available to anyone suffering substandard education are difficult to enforce and inadequate. The analysis surely serves to show that the quality control system is not yet so robust and well-founded that it can be relied upon to ensure what it is supposed to ensure, for employers and students alike.

On the positive side, this raises the fundamental question of whether the current, inadequate system can be reformed centrally, or whether a more radical, market-based solution is the only way forward. In the next sections, we look at recent developments by the Funding Councils and HEQC, and then consider outline policy solutions which embody all the elements which would be required, at least formally, for a solution of the problem. Readers may then judge for themselves the extent to which these centrally planned solutions could possibly be effective. Or perhaps it will be decided that they point to the inadvisability of attempting to use centrally-planned solutions for quality control of something as complex as higher education, especially with the added complexity of modularisation.

Developments by the Funding Councils and HEQC

The variety between different degrees at different institutions has been recognised in the Funding Councils' approach to teaching quality by concentrating its attention on a 'self-assessment' document, which the institution produces prior to an assessment visit in a given subject area: the intention then is to see how well the aims underlying the self-assessment are realised in practice.

The most recent specification for quality assessment of teaching provision came into effect from April 1995. Six aspects of provision are identified, each of which will be graded from 1 (aims not met, major shortcomings) to 4 (full contribution to attainment of stated objectives):

- curriculum design, content and organisation

- teaching, learning and assessment

- student progression and achievement

- student support and guidance

- learning resources

- quality assurance and enhancement.

It is clear that the intention is to encompass the variety of aim and provision without imposing judgements of value as to the 'objectives' themselves – the judgement is essentially confined to their realisation.

However, the work recently begun by the HEQC is more directly relevant. The question posed, in a study under the direction of Dr Peter Wright, is simply 'What are graduates?' and his paper (HEQC, 1996) is intended to initiate a very necessary discussion with institutions. The present paper has been produced independently of the HEQC group but it is hoped that it may contribute usefully to the discussion process.

Alternative Policy in the Context of Modular Education

The approach taken here is different from that of the HEQC study in that an attempt is made to address the question of 'graduateness' within a wider context of higher education policy. It has to be said that the following are not fully worked policies. The complexity of the factors involved in policy formation will become evident. The intention here is to indicate some directions which may prove useful.

First, any approach to higher education policy must fully recognise not only that modularity is an integral part of the scene but that the scene must be described in terms appropriate to modularity. It is not adequate to regard modularity as a down-market add-on to conventional modes. At the same time, the policy must protect (or at least not drive out) those traditional modes: their continuance is necessary for benchmarking of both quality and funding.

Add to this the requirement that education policy needs to recognise the time scales inherent in education (and in the institutional providers) and it becomes evident that complexity is not the only factor. Insofar as a generalised approach is possible, that suggested here is as follows. The adoption of modularity fragments education into modules that are diverse as to subject, level, provision, purpose and quality. These modules are then aggregated into courses (or 'programmes') which are so diverse in aim and outcome that to obtain an understanding of the whole by looking at (say) the aggregate of degree courses is essentially impossible: it is just not true that 'a degree is a degree', even within a broad subject category. Instead, an understanding of the activity in that category should be sought by looking for common or widespread 'threads' in that aggregate. It is then hoped that the 'bundling' of those threads will be sufficiently describable to make possible:

- an explicit categorisation of aspects (for instance, of the objectives of degree programmes) that will be useful for policy-makers and planners;

- a useful (that is, not too misleading) simplification of the categorisation which would be useful for prospective students and for employers, so that the market can be properly informed when making choices;

- a corresponding funding mechanism which is felt to be 'fair' across the huge diversity of higher education activity and is also capable of meeting a wide and variable set of policy objectives, so that control and influence can be exercised if so decided;

- a 'vision' tenable at the institutional level which assists in setting, explaining and achieving aims and objectives and which generates a marketing framework for the institution.

This is a specification for a meta-model of higher education which is daunting.

Explicit Categorisation of Objectives

We start with the discouraging realisation that there is (often profound) disagreement between institutions, between disciplines, and between professional and other bodies on the nature and balance of objectives. This realisation highlights the importance of making explicit those objectives – the 'threads' and 'strands' making up a degree – and bringing judgement to bear on them.

The approach taken embraces some of the arguments of those who advocate 'student profiles' – certifying what the student has done rather than giving a simple degree certificate. However, the problem with student profiles is that they are not user-friendly for the employer, that standards are not evident and that the balance is heavily towards complexity of statement. The operational scheme proposed looks forward to the new climate brought about by a fusing of the quality assurance and quality assessment systems, incorporating also the expertise of external examiners to calibrate the system.

The top 'tier' of the scheme would be a national 'agreement' (or, more realistically, a central specification imposed after discussion) as to the main quality strands which are important to the degree system but which contribute to different degrees to different extents. Of course, some strands (for example, one capable of being used to guarantee a threshold minimum of academic involvement) might be held to contribute to all.

A subsidiary tier of national 'agreement' arising from discussions, perhaps centred around each of the academic subject categories (ASCs) used for funding, would seek to achieve a further specification of quality strands for degrees awarded primarily in that ASC: for example, in Engineering and Technology, a strand relating to professional expertise would be appropriate as recognising an objective which appears in many (but not all) engineering degree programmes. This tier would involve the relevant professional and statutory bodies and main employers.

A third tier might be appropriate to accommodate the various local, regional and other networks of institutions. This tier would (for example) harness the expertise on standards developed by the various associations of credit-awarding bodies but should not influence the higher tiers directly.

Overall, the aim would be to provide a framework that would be just complex enough to accommodate diversity of mission but simple enough to be capable of relating to the needs of the market for clear information on the quality and the nature of a particular degree programme.

Let us take Engineering as an example. It might be that the main strands identified as potentially important were (these are illustrative only):

- academic standards in core subjects;

- management and knowledge of the industry;

- problem solving and project work;

- information handling and computer proficiency;

- group work and communication skills.

It would then be for each educational institution to rate these strands in its Engineering courses and to publish these ratings in prospectus and other publicity material. The ratings would in principle be absolute (that is, not a statement of relative importance) and would be intended to quantify the standard of achievement by graduates from the course in each strand, measured (say) at the boundary between a 2(ii) and 2(i) degree, or in some other standardisable way.

There would need to be a nationally-agreed scale for this rating. The quality rating scale used for research assessment by the funding councils in the Research Assessment Exercise provides an example (but not a wholly transferable model) of such a scale. In effect, this would be an institutional 'self-assessment' – but one which used nationally agreed headings (the 'strands') and standards (the scale) and one which was made public independently of any teaching assessment visit. On such a visit, however, the institution would be assessed against the ratings which it had claimed in its publicity material, taking into account the written views of external examiners as to whether the implied standards had been achieved.

A system which was explicit in this way would admit great diversity but would provide information to the 'market' on what the choices really meant.

Of course, many objections can be raised against such a system. For example, the teaching assessment process is slow and institutions could publish over-optimistic claims for several years without check. Also, if funding is linked (as will be proposed) to these claims, the teaching assessment visits could become very uncomfortable confrontations. It would therefore be advisable to develop the system in such a way that new claims made by institutions would be limited (through an added HEQC mechanism) to an assessment based on their historical record of achievement and on their capability to provide in each subject area and at each level.

But most crucially, the objection may be that such a system would be as cumbersome, unworkable, and as educationally inadequate as the current system. The purpose of outlining it here is to show that it is only this sort of route which *could* satisfy the desire for quality control within the state-directed system, in particular one moving towards modularity. If this sort of route is not feasible, then we would have to look to more radical solutions.

The latest evidence from the funding councils is that the state-directed system of quality control will seek to reduce diversity of provision, rather than tackle the full complexities outlined above. They propose instead to develop a 'typology' of courses, restricting their funding to a limited range of approved types. The intention is to begin with postgraduate courses – that is, precisely those where student choice and modularity should be allowed fullest rein.

4 | Funding

This chapter focuses on three issues concerned with the debate about the future of higher education funding on which modularisation has an impact. *First*, it points to the unsustainability of the current system of funding. *Second*, ways of filling the funding gap are explored, many of which point to the viability of modularisation. *Third*, some modifications to the current funding system are outlined which could facilitate flexibility, including moves towards modularisation.

Present Funding and the Student Experience

In the UK, the level of funding per student has been falling steadily: from about £6,900 per full-time equivalent student in 1989-90 to about £4,400 in 1997-98 (DfEE 1996). In part, of course, this reflects the expansion in the student population from about 580,000 full-time equivalent (fte) to nearly a million. Even though this 'headline' figure of per-student cost ignores the shift in the student mix from more-expensive to less-expensive (non-science) subjects during the expansion, it is a very significant reduction. It is unrealistic to expect this trend to be reversed, even if the present lobbying by the Vice-Chancellors succeeds in arresting the decline. There are therefore serious doubts about whether traditional full-time intensive courses, based on a lecture/tutorial mix with some individual support, can survive without unacceptable diminution in the quality and variety of the student experience. Indeed, there is a strong case for saying that the diminution in provision has already reached the point of unacceptability. Hence, the way students are currently funded now brings strong pressures for modularisation.

There is space for only one brief demonstration. If we take a subject like Business and Management, the (England) Average Unit of Council Funding for 1993/94 is £1,190. To this – for an undergraduate – is added fee income of £750 through the Mandatory Award system, together with a fee compensation element from the HEFCE of £560. The total is

£2,500 per (home/European Community) student. Of the £2,500 total, about 35-40 per cent characteristically goes in infrastructure support: computers, premises, library, administration, student facilities. The departmental spend is what remains – say, £1,500. This spend is very largely (about 80 per cent) on academic staff. Estimating their average salary (including employer's salary costs) to be about £37,000 gives a *teaching only* student-staff ratio of just over 30.[1]

The consequences of this ratio for teaching group size are obvious. A traditional full-time undergraduate course requires perhaps 12 hours per week student contact over 30 weeks. Even if there were no other lectures or tutorials whatsoever, one hour of individual tuition per week would generate (from the group of 30 students funding a single member of staff) a requirement for 900 hours of teaching, almost double the amount of teaching which can be extracted from a teaching-only member of academic staff during a three-term year. In practice, therefore, academic staff can be afforded only if they (almost) always teach in large groups.

This puts acute pressure on activities such as supervision of individual projects, which are generally regarded as highly valuable in encouraging a student's personal development. Group projects therefore tend to be substituted but – though these encourage other qualities such as working in a team – their worth as an evaluative mechanism is questionable. A further aspect is the virtual disappearance of the 'informal tutorial', where the student can get individual help from a lecturer outside the timetable.

Although the argument in this section has been developed for a particular subject category, the results are generalisable to all categories except Medicine, Dentistry, Veterinary Science, and Teacher Education where student numbers are state controlled. Also, because of the argument developed below (see Appendix B) that the unit of resource is near-uniform (after weighted averaging within each institution over all subject categories), the 'traditional' universities (with the present exceptions of Oxford and

---

[1] The figure of 19 given for 1993/94 in CVCP statistics for 'old' universities (CVCP, 1994, Table 1:32) is misleading as a comparison since it includes the effect of research funding and of overseas students' fees, which are of the order of £5,000.

Cambridge[2]) cannot stand aloof.

It might be thought that this substantial funding gap could be addressed by finding alternative sources of funding for higher education. In the next section we briefly review five possibilities for plugging this gap, in the context of undergraduate education.

Addressing the Funding Gap in Undergraduate Courses

The possibilities considered here involve the following five:

1. A move away from full-time to part-time modes in which state-funded maintenance grants are not required or can be reduced, with transfer of saving to pay more for tuition.

2. Additional ('top-up') tuition fees from the student.

3. Reducing research funding to universities, switching the funding towards tuition.

4. Finding cheaper modes of delivery, in particular, those involving less intensive tuition.

5. Transferring some higher education to the further education sector.

These possibilities are related to those considered in a report to the CVCP by Williams and Fry (1994). The *first*, clearly, would favour the development of 'strong' modularity,

---

[2] It is already the case that Oxford and Cambridge are heavily protected from the general funding pressures because of the arrangements by which the college undergraduate fee (typically around £3,000 per annum) is paid through the mandatory award scheme. Although the HEFCE grant is reduced to take account of this, the reduction is not *pro rata* and the net benefit to each of these institutions is estimated as £10 million per annum at the 1989-90 UFC resource allocation, which has fed into the HEFCE processes; this represented about 10% of 'general recurrent' income. The effect has been to place those institutions most favourably in relation to the 'level playing field' on which other institutions are expected to compete according to formula funding. There is a multiplier effect both in respect of research funding and in regard to teaching quality, where there is intense support for students, albeit on a very short teaching year. Obviously, the *ad-hoc* protection that has been afforded to Oxford and Cambridge cannot realistically be extended to other institutions.

so that courses can be taken over a longer period than that of the traditional full-time course, with flexibility as to the part-time/full-time mix during that period, to accommodate the varying possibilities for employment during the course. The *second*, introducing top-up fees, may be politically hazardous for any Government. However, if income-contingent loans were introduced this might reduce the political unacceptability of universities charging such fees, particularly if such loans incorporated an element for fee payments. This would then bring undergraduate courses more into line with some postgraduate courses, where the operation of top-up fees for work-related courses is a well-accepted feature.[3]

Reducing research funding, the *third* possibility, and switching funds to teaching may not be a realistic alternative. Although research and teaching funding have now been efficiently separated, the separation for individual academic staff members may not be perceptible or even meaningful. For it is important to recognise a peculiarity of academic staff: their main loyalty is often to their subject discipline, rather than to their employing institution. For such staff, the opportunity and time to undertake research in that discipline are key elements of job satisfaction, explaining why academic salaries, though depressed, do not seem generally to interfere with recruitment and retention. This 'hidden subsidy' complicates policy-making.

However, the most cogent counter-argument is that it would not do enough to address the funding shortfall. Figures for 1994/95 are available and show that the total HEFCE funding for research was £626 million, compared with a total income for the sector of £8,190 million. Of this research funding, a third was associated with the top seven institutions (ranked in order of HEFCE research funding) out of about 100 on the main HEFCE list. Thus, even the extreme measure of limiting funding to those seven institutions would produce funds of only about £400 million (i.e., two-thirds of £626 million), to be spread over about one million fte students.

---

[3] Here, career loans can be obtained from banks and tax remission is generally available. The size of the top-up fee can be large, with total fees approaching £10,000 per full-time year for the best MBA courses, against the (1996) standard home postgraduate fee of £2,430. Such courses are operating in a market which is relatively undistorted by public funding.

Clearly, this is hardly enough seriously to address a funding gap measured in thousands of pounds per student. Anything less than this extreme measure will be even less effective.

The *fourth* scenario, of finding cheaper modes of delivery, can perhaps be introduced by reminding us of Dr Schnabel's dictum: when his astronomical charges for tuition (as the leading concert pianist of his day) were questioned, he replied: 'I *do* give cheaper lessons – but I do not recommend them.'

The challenge is to produce modes of study which are good of their kind, clearly identifiable as such, and which will be cheaper than the traditional modes of study. Clearly, modularity could have a key role to play. Modularity blurs the distinction between part-time and full-time modes of study: if a module is truly self-contained, there is no logical need to inquire what other modules are being taken at the same time. If students are to be fully in control of higher education as consumers, then they should be free to choose the balance between employment, leisure and work at any time. The reduction in time pressure and the reduced (or zero) penalties for failure mean that the student does not need such intensive tutorial support, even though guidance on module choice is required. Furthermore, modular courses tend to be less 'linear' than their traditional counterparts, in that building in detail upon previous sections is of less importance, so that there is a tendency to substitute breadth for depth. This means that a wide choice of options can be given to a student at any stage of the course, without the resource penalty of specialising into the small groups associated with advanced stages of the traditional course.

The counter-argument of the traditionalists is that academic 'pressure' is what good institutions impose on their students: the full-time traditional course is what distinguishes British honours degree education from its Continental and US rivals. Its intensiveness allows it to be short compared with the European norm of four years or more (three-year courses still account for over two-thirds of the market in old universities) and that helps to make it good value for the taxpayer, especially when completion rates are taken into account. Also, the need for linear development is especially strong in subjects like Mathematics if high output standards are to be achieved.

Modularity raises important and complex questions. The

proper conclusion is that it can indeed be used to construct cheaper and more flexible courses than the traditional route. These courses have the further advantage that the student can be credited with what he or she has managed to achieve, even if there is not full progression to degree level. However, the highest output standards in 'linear' subjects are not likely to be achieved (unless the choice of modules is severely restricted to be close to the structure of a cohort-based course).

Finally, could more use be made of what is called in the UK, the 'further education' (FE – colleges which normally offer high school-level and vocational qualifications) sector, to cut the costs of higher education? Already there is some co-operation between these sectors, with, for example, 'Access' courses conducted in FE colleges. Also, there are already in place 'franchising' arrangements, principally but not exclusively relating to the 'foundation years', which are provided for Engineering and other 'hard science' courses. The saving on funds comes because the average unit of resource is lower in FE than in higher education (though it is misleading to compare averages over all years in such a simple way, because the costs in universities tend to be higher in later years of the course).

Extending the use of FE provision in these and similar ways is a genuine possibility, though there are concerns about whether higher education institutions are properly supervising the franchise arrangements and about the quality of student experience. Making the transitions between FE and higher education more seamless would be necessary (and not easy, given the wide variety of FE qualifications and courses): institutions which span the two sectors would be at an advantage here.

While many of the options may seem unattractive, the discussion here has suggested that scenarios 2 and 3 ('top-up' tuition fees for students, and switching research funding towards tuition) would not be politically viable unless, the crucial caveat, income-contingent loans were introduced for higher education. However, scenarios 1, 4 and 5 (moving from full-time to part-time modes; finding cheaper modes of delivery; and transferring some higher education to the further education sector) all have their strengths, and all, interestingly, point to the viability of moving towards modularisation.

Furthermore, these different possibilities could bring about opportunities for institutions to develop in *three* distinctive ways. *First,* institutions could move towards the provision of low-intensity modular education at correspondingly low cost. *Second,* some institutions could develop study-intensive courses for suitable students, compressing three years into two (say).[4] *Finally,* some institutions would seek to demonstrate that at least some of the traditional courses are capable of giving good value for money when funded at the above-average 'intensive' rate, taking into account high output standards, high objectives and high completion rates.

To achieve such a redistribution of funding will inevitably mean making hard distinctions between (comparatively) well-funded activities and (comparatively) cheap activities. It is an entirely legitimate process for funding councils to make such distinctions, in the name of public policy, just as is now done for research. However, the councils will need to build a capability to judge and evaluate. An interesting question is whether this in practice means making such distinctions and evaluations not just at the course level, or even at the level of the institutional sub-unit such as a school or department, but also at the level of the institution.

Alternative Funding Mechanisms

We now turn to address alternative funding mechanisms, in particular, exploring ways in which these could be made more flexible to accommodate the requirements of modularity. The prescription sought is that of a 'fair' funding system which is capable of meeting a wide range of policy objectives, including the proper funding of a diversity of (properly labeled) modular courses.

Problems in Funding of Alternative Modes of Study

There is widespread discontent, including from HEFCE itself (HEFCE, 1996), with the present funding régime, which is felt to be too inflexible, creating artificial barriers between

---

[4] Particularly if this was coupled with changes in the mandatory grant arrangements to give such students a higher rate of grant/loan so that they can truly study in an intensive mode, or with the introduction of income-contingent loans which could be used in similar ways.

different modes of study, and not facilitating moves towards modularisation. One root of the problem is that there is no robust procedure for converting part-time study into full-time equivalents for funding comparison purposes. This has now been addressed by HEFCE and, from 1996/97, a (fairly crude) comparison measure is being collected with institutional statistics. This measure is based on expected time to complete the part-time alternative, as compared with the expected time to complete the full-time course leading to the equivalent qualification. Even this, though, falls short of a system robust enough to withstand the 'Gresham's Law' pressure to devalue provision. Gresham's Law says that bad money drives out good. Its application here is that if, for the achievement of a given qualification, a cheap alternative mode of study is found, the institution providing it will derive benefits relative to other institutions providing more expensive modes. In a genuine market, this would not matter, because (at least some) consumers would be well informed about what they were getting (in terms of quality and quantity) for their money and could choose accordingly; with a core of such responsible consumers, quality need not suffer.

However, without such genuine market mechanisms, the structure of the funding model creates a very different background; and the existence of a national framework itself creates the expectation that all provision will be at least of adequate quality. It is therefore necessary for the funding council to take decisions about what segmentation is appropriate in the artificial market which it creates. How far should full-time courses compete against part-time? Should distance learning courses have a separate category? Yet, in the world of modularity, these distinctions are difficult (or impossible) to draw.

Indeed, in that world, the concept of whether a *course* (as opposed to a module) is offered in a particular mode has no meaning. It is possible to say whether a given *student* has achieved the required standard in various modules constituting the course leading to the award by full-time study, part-time study, distance learning, or by exemption (recognising that these descriptions may be combined as fractions not just as integers) – but this is the language of an individual student transcript, not a description applicable to a cohort. The implications are profound.

Robertson's Over-arching Proposals

The Robertson Report (HEQC, 1994) clearly recognises the need for some form of over-arching funding model to address the problem of funding all modes of study fairly. However, the idea contained in the report that such a model can be based almost entirely on the notion of 'credits' is – as will be demonstrated – too simple. As summarised in the Executive Statement (recommendation 9), the report proposes:

> The creation of a national credit framework based on a structure of level of attainment, a common unit of credit and credit currency, agreed interim awards and a shared approach to definitions of achievement. The framework would embrace not only conventional higher and further education but also all appropriate, assessable learning wherever acquired. The report envisages that progress initially will depend on an articulation of the existing different systems of credit currency leading by a process of convergence to a unified credit framework in due course. It stresses a bottom-up acceptance and adoption of shared understandings and common definitions of what constitutes credit-based learning rather than a top-down, prescriptive, centralised model.

The response to this part of the report (HEQC, 1995) is at best guarded. Though institutionally-based credit accumulation and transfer is felt to be acceptable and is to be encouraged, a distinction is made between that and a supra-institutional credit framework, which is felt to be more contentious and more open to misunderstanding. However, there is 'widespread concern' for consistency of credit rating, for a commonality of definition and understanding as regards 'levels' of learning achieved. Further, though there is support neither for a centrally-imposed unitary system of credit overseen by a central bureaucracy, nor for the complete reorganisation along credit-based lines, there is support for the emergence by alignment or articulation of an agreed unified system, based on an 'institutionally-owned credit culture'. Whether such a structure could emerge or evolve without at least some central 'light steer' is, according to the document, 'a matter for consideration'.

A further key recommendation of the report is to establish credit-based funding as the organisational arrangement for the allocation and distribution of funds. This recommendation was fairly widely supported by educational institutions –

about one-third did so, with another third giving qualified support, though there was a wide range of concerns about the detail, and impact of the particular proposals of the report. The professional and statutory bodies consulted were less supportive. The consultation on the Robertson report set out above shows that credit-led funding is by no means felt to be a non-starter. It is therefore of interest to demonstrate its unsuitability.

Unsuitability of Credit-Based Funding

The suggestion in the Robertson report is that funding (for all modes of study) should be based upon credit equivalence within a universal credit-rating scheme, so that the unit of credit becomes a 'unit of account' for the system. The difficulties with this suggestion are:

- that credit rating is fundamentally distinct from teaching provision;

- that credit rating is not robust.

The concept of credit rating is attractively, and deceptively, simple: that different learning experiences can be quantified in terms of some unit of credit. Thus, if a course leading to a given qualification (say, an honours degree) is divided into self-contained modules, it should be possible to assign a points value to each module (not necessarily the same for each) adding up to an agreed total for the degree. *These 'credit ratings' are then taken to have a more universal validity, so that they can be used to determine whether a different combination of modules (taken from different courses and even different institutions) is itself worth a degree.*

The italicised statement requires justification. Thus, there needs first to be an agreed operational procedure for determining the credit ratings; and, further, the additivity of the ratings must be proved to be useful by empirical trial. It is perhaps worth stressing that the concept of *additivity of consistent measures* which is being put forward is very problematic. If consistency of quantification is not achievable within some set of 'best practice' procedures, then the concept may need to be re-thought or even abandoned. Or, it may be that the concept will prove consistent only within some restricted range of learning experiences; application of it outside that range may be possible with modifications – or may be positively misleading. Consistency is only one requirement. The quantification must also be useful, whether to assist in evaluating an aggregation of learning experiences, or in distributing resources, or to foster the codifying and organisation of different learning systems. It would take us too far to enter into a detailed description of credit rating and its problems. Suffice it to say that the programme of validation of the concept has not been adequately carried out. Various approaches have been tried to establish consistent ratings:

- by reference to the (judgementally assigned) weighting of units within the overall award (CNAA);

- by reference to time spent by the student (CNAA, ECTIS) but allowing judgementally for differences arising, for example, from work-based placements;

- by determining the 'notional time' to achieve a defined set of learning outcomes (FEU).

It should be evident that the judgemental elements in all these render them unsafe and non-auditable for funding allocation purposes, particularly when it is recognised that the judgements are performed by the institutions themselves within their capacity as self-validating bodies.

This is not intended to damn credit accumulation and transfer (CAT) schemes in themselves. Credit rating within a credit accumulation and transfer scheme was of course introduced in this country by the CNAA, which acted as a central validating body for the then polytechnic sector. That circumstance provided a number of useful safeguards, contributing greatly to the (fairly) general acceptance of credit rating (as a rough-and-ready tool) for the purposes of award of diploma, first degree and taught masters qualifications. Even though some post-CNAA developments are more questionable in regard to acceptability of standards, most institutions – as the outcomes document indicates – will expect to credit rate most if not all their courses in future.

Provision-Based Funding

The Robertson report contains the outline of an alternative funding model (contributed by the present author but somewhat modified in the report itself) which would base funding on *teaching provision* within each specified module and so would recognise that the funding councils are purchasers of teaching, not of learning credit. The suggestion, put simply, is that: *institutions should be paid according to the kind of educational provision they supply and the numbers of students taught, in any particular module,* not according to the advance in learning it produces for the student who completes the module successfully.

A word, though, is necessary about the phrase 'provision-based' – a phrase which tends to raise hackles in the Department for Education and Employment (DfEE). It could easily be misinterpreted as meaning: 'we will pay the institution if it delivers (say) twenty lectures' without regard to quality of or need for the provision. But quality is a key part of provision.

It is convenient to approach the development of a provision-based funding model from the standpoint of the existing Higher Education Funding Council for England (HEFCE) 'funding model'.[5] HEFCE, charged with the task of unifying the University and Polytechnic sectors, has chosen a model in which the main determinant of an institution's teaching funding for a given activity in a given year is its teaching funding in the previous year. Movement towards the system median cost is encouraged in two ways:

- by imposing a differential reduction in the institution's unit of resource, graduated according to the institution's position in the league table of expenditure; and

- by selective allocation of additional funded numbers (if any) to the cheaper institutions.

For this purpose, teaching activity is divided into 11

---

[5] A 'funding model' may be defined as a means of allocating funds to institutions in which not all the decisions are determined by direct human judgement; instead, there is an arithmetic mechanism whereby judgements (such as policy decisions) are fed in as rules with appropriate parameters derived from overall resource constraints and from the performance statistics of individual institutions. The aim is that yearly funding outcomes shall be transparent – either mechanistic from year to year or subject to well-defined policy changes – and hence seen to be 'fair' by institutions.

academic subject categories, each of which is further split *four* ways: between full-time and part-time modes, and between taught course and research course levels. There is thus a separate system-wide competition for funds in each of 44 (11 x 4) 'cells'. Failure (through under-recruitment or excessive dropout and academic withdrawal) to achieve funded number targets is punished by proportionate clawback of grant in-year, with consequential effects on funding in subsequent years, though this clawback is mitigated by the possibility of 'inter-cell virement' (subject to certain rules, for example those preventing the substitution of numbers on hard science courses by others), and by safety-net arrangements.[6]

There are a number of tests which any new funding model will need to satisfy if it is to pass muster with the HEFCE:

- The mechanism should provide the Funding Council with the same possibilities for control and influence as at present.

- It should be possible to replicate existing funding as a 'special case'.

- In particular, 'traditional' provision should not be threatened, other than by healthy competition, and the institutions concerned should not be forced to adopt alien modes.

- There should be no hidden policy implications – for example, it should not 'drive' the system to a new pattern of provision unless that is a conscious policy decision.

- The mechanism should be (relatively) simple and fully transparent.

---

[6] It is interesting that this model is bringing the system quite closely back to the UGC system of uniform units of resource, albeit at a much lower level, and for teaching only (see Appendix A). Thus an analysis of university funding (Appendix B) indicates that for the main multi-disciplinary institutions, the total allocation of full-time teaching resource (grant plus fee) is already 98 per cent correlated with that which would be allocated under uniform units of resource, though of course there are discrepancies of allocation within institutions between different subjects. (It is not possible to perform the same analysis in respect of other modes of teaching, because of limitations in the published information.)

- The cost of implementation to the Funding Council and to the institutions should not be increased significantly.

- The relationships between Government, the Department for Education and Employment, the Funding Councils and Institutions of Higher Education should not be forced into radical change.

- Implications for the mandatory award system and/or other forms of student support should be separable.

These are formidable constraints – and others could be added to the list. However, the list is long enough for the present purpose, which is to explore the obstacles for alternative funding models, and consider possible ways round them. Some of these entail compromises; others could well improve the present system in its own right.

In the proposed new funding scheme *funding by academic subject category* would be simplified down from the 11 categories mentioned above to (say) the following five, based on the kind of educational provision that was being made:

- low-cost/no-laboratory;

- high-cost/no-laboratory;

- computer based;

- laboratory/practical;

- clinical.

The unit costs of programmes in each academic subject category would then depend on the mix of module costs. There is, of course, no requirement that modules be equal in length or in credit.

Implementation of this mechanism would require a re-apportionment exercise similar in principle to that undertaken by the HEFCE each year, requiring institutions to apportion their present teaching income as between the various elements within programmes. Given guidance on overhead attribution, such an exercise is far from impossible. It would also be possible to set or indicate minimum standards of provision – for instance, how much 'laboratory' should be in a module classified at the laboratory rate – in a more precise way than at present. *Funding by level* could well remain as at present, differentiating between taught courses (undergraduate and postgraduate) and research courses, though there is an argument for differentiating taught course levels more finely, especially since the undergraduate and postgraduate fees are not uniform, and since the costs of provision at undergraduate level vary considerably as between first, second and final years.

So far, there are no insuperable problems: the funding that would result would differ in detail from the present, but there would be smoothing out at the institutional level. The complexity has been reduced overall (from 11x4 to 5x2) and there is attraction in the new categorisations, which are not explicitly subject-based.

Funding by mode is where the first real problem arises. In a fully-modular system, there is no such thing as 'mode'. As has been said above, it is only possible to say whether the student is 'full-time' or 'part-time' by looking at the individual's learning contract. It is not a natural question to ask at institutional level. This strongly suggests that the present question, 'what mode is the student in on his/her course?' would be replaced by the only meaningful question, 'what teaching/learning mode is the module in?'.

The kind of distinction between modes that might be useful would be:

- intensive tuition;

- normal tuition;

- student-centred learning with some tutorial supervision;

- full-distance learning;

with definitions that would guarantee minimum standards of provision appropriate to each category.

Those four modes would then be introduced into the 5x2 matrix of cells identified above, giving a final total of 40 cells (i.e. 5x2x4) for the funding model. This compares favourably with the 44 cells of the current funding model. Hence, the interesting conclusion is that a provision-based funding mechanism could be devised, with the above compromises/improvements, which would not be significantly more complicated, in terms of funding cells, than the present one. Furthermore, the categorisation of courses by teaching/learning mode is much more defensible as an institutional funding parameter than is the present full-time/part-time student categorisation, especially when it is recognised that both kinds of student can often be found attending the same module.

The proposed method of funding has the great advantage that it combines funding of traditional and non-traditional provision in a way that is 'fair' (non-distortional) and is free from the 'Gresham's Law' objections mentioned earlier. Also, there is full continuity of funding (through the reapportionment mechanism) with the present HEFCE model. Nor is there any difficulty in principle in applying the present 'core plus margin' allocation method of funded student numbers to cells.

Two difficulties may be urged against the new proposals, however. At the institutional level, the institution would be required, subject to virement, to meet funded student number targets in the cells, as implied by Funding Council allocations. Yet an institution going for a full student-empowered modular scheme has much less control of these numbers than under a cohort-based system (in which admissions to the different programmes control the cell numbers more-or-less effectively). However, this problem is not caused by the funding model. It is a consequence of student empowerment and choice, which are assumed to be desirable. The severity of the problem is a matter for institutional decision, since there is nothing (except market forces) to stop an institution from restricting that choice. Institutions that use full CAT schemes are even now aware of the management problems of working within an internal/external market. The proposed funding methodology would present no extra complications.

The second difficulty is at the Funding Council level. If the Council wishes to encourage more distance-learning provision, it can do so: cells are provided. Similarly, if it wishes to encourage more laboratory or computer-based activity, there are cells. However, encouragement of part-time provision as against full-time is not possible: it is not just the absence of cells – the distinction has gone from the system. Likewise, encouragement of specific academic subject categories becomes an indirect exercise; though it would, of course, be possible to except entire programmes – such as clinical medicine – from the modular scheme. It is indeed arguable that these changes in the influence of the Funding Council are appropriate: but they do represent a definite change of approach.

The conclusions of this section are that it would be preferable to use the proposed 'provision-based' funding model to mediate the transition of the system to new modes of study. In that way, traditional courses (and their institutions) would have the best chance of survival against unfair funding competition – but not a guarantee of survival, if the new modes of study or other institutions ultimately proved more attractive and cost-effective in the market-place.

Dangers of Output-related Funding and 'Value Added' Measures

There is only space for a brief word on output-related funding. Put simply, the suggestion is that institutions should be paid according to the output of successful 'completers' of a module rather than the numbers of students taught. Obviously, this could be incorporated as a variant of the above model by saying: *institutions should be paid according to the kind of educational provision they supply and the numbers of students successfully completing, in any particular module.*

This is not a fundamental change, though it can have substantial operational consequences. It puts a direct funding pressure against maintenance of standards. However, not to make the change encourages institutions to take in students who cannot reasonably be expected to complete. In practice, the Funding Councils strike a balance by paying for students who complete – in the sense of completing the assessment(s) of the year or semester – even if they do not complete successfully.

It is necessary to point out that this benign compromise does not address the public policy questions arising from high drop-out rates in degree programmes. Even where the year or semester is completed, the outcome may be that the student does not meet the standard required to continue at degree level. Some institutions then give lower-level awards (such as undergraduate diplomas or certificates) but it is questionable whether these have much educational value or utility in the employment market.

The concept of funding by *value added* is more subtle. Here, the institution is to be paid according to the increase in educational 'value' for the student arising from (successful) completion of the module. More would be paid if the student started from a low 'value' than from a high. This basis is attractive to those institutions which take in substantial numbers of educationally disadvantaged students. It is less attractive to institutions which take in very bright and educationally advantaged students, not for any fundamental reason – both categories may be difficult to teach successfully – but because (it is argued) the top end of educational attainment is open-ended and is not properly measured by a simple scale which gives 'points' for the class of degree.

The problem is not dissimilar to that encountered in the measurement of credit. The difficulty is compounded in that suitable measures (additive, standardised and robust) are needed both for input and for output. Bearing in mind the great diversity of inputs likely in a modular system, it is hard to envisage any auditable system emerging. However, the linearisation of output measures in higher education is an interesting topic in its own right. Measures used for classification of degrees – such as weighted aggregate percentages, or combinations of rank orders – are notoriously unsuitable in this respect.

However, though 'value added' is not a sufficiently robust measure to be used for funding, the concept is useful in describing such things as the mission or market placing of an institution or educational programme.

The HEFCE Consultation on the Funding Method for Teaching

The consultation paper on the funding method for teaching issued by the HEFCE (HEFCE, 1996) proposes several of the features of the scheme put forward by the present author:

- provision-based funding with standard prices;

- a simple set of price groups on to which subjects would be mapped according to the nature of provision (clinical, laboratory, part-laboratory, classroom) but recognising that in an increasingly modular system most students would be taught in more than one price-group.

There would also be weighting by mode, though the characteristics (full-time, part-time, distance-learning) indicate that the HEFCE has not been able to accept entirely the implications of modularity. The root of this is that full-time undergraduates and part-time undergraduates need to be accounted for separately, principally because the eligibility of (some) full-time students for Local Authority maintenance grants requires a separate control on numbers for that category of student.

A new proposal in the consultation paper is for a positive weight to be given to 'non-standard' undergraduate students, particularly students with disabilities and many mature students; undergraduates from socio-economic groups III-V would also be positively weighted.

One feature which is absent (apart from the separate funding weight for distance learning) is the possibility of establishing funding differentials between various possible intensities of provision (for example, 'intensive', 'normal' and 'student-centred' provision of tuition). However, this feature is essential to a system of funding if it is to be capable of properly recognising diversity, and this particular need for differential provision (funding which is sensitive to the intensity of tuition) arises from the financial pressures on the expanding system. Here the word 'intensity' is used to cover a number of different possibilities of high-cost provision: tuition in small groups, high-immersion courses, courses especially well supported by laboratories, and tailored computer-based learning support all come to mind.[7]

---

[7] At the time of writing, the HEFCE was modifying its proposals to give additional funding to courses taught for more than 45 weeks in the year.

5 | Evolution of Institutions in the Higher Education System

This paper has set out the basic tenets of the modularisation debate. After analysing the main components of traditional, cohort-based higher education and those of modularised education, we showed how there are strong pressures for modularisation within higher education. These pressures could lead to a more responsive, efficient and consumer-driven higher education system, rather than the producer-driven system which exists at present.

However, two crucial issues arise. First, how can quality be maintained within a modularised higher education system; and second, how can funding of students take place in such a system? On the first, we showed that the current quality control system is in any case suspect, unlikely to ensure quality even without the pressures which modularisation brings to bear. An alternative model of quality control was tentatively suggested – in full awareness that its complexity too may make it unworkable, and may in fact lead to pressures for a quality control system outside any central planning mechanisms. Concerning the second issue, of funding, we showed that the current funding model for higher education is simply untenable. However, modularisation could move some way towards improving funding options, by creating flexibility in costs and student demand where at present there can be none. (A system of income contingent loans would also go some way to easing these funding pressures). Finally, we showed how within a system of government funds for teaching, flexibility is feasible, enhancing the prospects of moving towards a modularised system.

It will not be easy for institutions – given existing funding régimes and policies – to resist the pressures identified and discussed in this paper. There is the general pressure to go with those universities, led by the ex-polytechnics, which have decided to modularise. A university would need to be clear as to the consequences of resisting. Student marketing might be adversely affected because of the (illusion of?) choice presented by modular schemes elsewhere. There may be marketing niches for institutions which offer traditional courses, at least at undergraduate level where their market is predominantly full-time students – the low quality of the experience of full-time students on some modular schemes designed for part-time and credit accumulation would reinforce this possibility. However, the funding pressures are at present all one way: to reduce the intensity of the course and the tutorial support. This could ultimately drive out the traditional courses.

The proposal here would seek to mitigate that possibility. Under it, all institutions would compete for teaching funding. Some institutions would achieve this by demonstrating high output standards and would correspondingly need to attract students capable of benefiting from intensive tuition. Other institutions would achieve it by demonstrating success with intensive tuition for educationally-disadvantaged students and would be rewarded accordingly.

Given that the quality ratings for courses would be explicit and that information about the emphasis and achievement of each course would be available, there may appear to be no reason in principle why the marketing of institutions should not be course-based: the information is there for the market to judge. The same institution could thus offer a highly demanding course in one subject, with restrictive entry, but could also offer a wide open course with relatively low standards of output in another subject area.

In practice, this is what universities do at present: entry standards vary enormously as between subjects in high demand and low demand. However, it makes the institution extremely difficult to market, both to students and to employers, and quite difficult to run, because of lack of shared internal values. A coherent marketing image of, say, 'excellence' or 'openness' cannot be projected.

As institutions become more competitive in the educational 'market', these tensions become harder to live with. It is therefore likely that institutions wishing to survive will find themselves under pressure to restrict their range of activity in order to achieve greater marketing coherence and provide a reasonably uncluttered 'vision'. Furthermore, as teaching quality assessment proceeds with greater rigour and transparency, some institutions will find it exceedingly difficult to aspire to the full range of provision.

This process of specialisation in the market and the development of a corresponding image is at once recognisable as the formation of a brand. A good brand, once formed, must of course be maintained by rigorous attention to standards inside the institution. This opens up the possibility that in those circumstances much of the control of quality and standards could safely be returned to the institutional level, thus avoiding the undesirable aspects of central bureaucratic control outlined at the end of Chapter 3.

The Funding Councils need to prepare for this and to provide evolution pathways for institutions in transition. Most institutions, given the history of 'underfunding' (expenditure exceeding income, after properly allowing for depreciation and maintenance of premises), do not have reserves which would allow them to make such transitions.

Where will all this lead? It may be argued that the traditional full-time course should not be written off prematurely, even though the signs of strain are clearly visible. After all, a policy of the kind outlined above appears to provide a set of niches for a high-quality 'conventional' university, concerned about the possible adverse consequences of radical change on its undergraduate activity. The university can always modularise and credit rate its undergraduate courses, in order to 'appear more progressive'. But the danger of adopting this defensive stance is that it assumes a static view of undergraduate entrance to higher education. In that view, the university has been seen essentially as the chief bridge between school and high-quality jobs. Now, with increasing participation rates, with the growth of post-experiential learning and post-qualification vocational education, the scene is complex and interest – including from government – is turning to the bridging role of the further education sector. The evolutionary pressures on that diverse sector are even more strong than those on the universities.

Perhaps, if the consequences of letting the evolutionary forces have full play are recognised, there will be a rearguard action by the traditional universities, possibly operating through the HEQC, since the CVCP is too fundamentally split on these issues to form an effective pressure group. But this raises the crucial question, of how many 'traditional' universities can be afforded? The underlying concern about inadequacy of state funding in a mass system is likely to remain, whatever devices are used to minimise the problem.

Only if those universities seize the nettle of deriving extra income from the market will they be able to break clear as an élite from the mass system. To do that, they will require clear strategies to define and distinguish what is meant by an élite education so that it can be marketed – starting, in all probability, from the perception which students have that a 'proper degree' is a traditional full-time degree. They will also have to operate in ways contrary to their in-built preference for entry based on ability, rather than on ability to pay. And some of them may come to realise that a system based on a student's purchasing power is one in which a student has real power as a purchaser. After all, what is being sold in this élite layer is the ideal of higher education: the interaction of a good, though untrained, mind, with that of a scholar of distinction. How genuine is that interaction nowadays?

It is doubtful whether all the top traditional universities, given their 'collegiate' ethos, have the management coherence to implement an aggressive strategy of this kind, especially if it runs counter to political sensitivities. Nevertheless, even if the mechanisms are unclear at present, it is likely that the adoption of a mass system of higher education in the UK will, as in other countries, stimulate the overt development of an élite layer, one which indeed gains lustre by comparison with the rest.

Below this, a second layer of institutions may start to identify themselves as concerned with professional education in the wide sense. Here, the influence of the professional bodies, such as the Engineering Council, or the General Optical Council, acts to prevent standards of provision falling below well-defined minima. For such institutions, the challenge will be to demonstrate the effectiveness of relatively intensive provision in achieving output standards related to professional requirements. They will need to be imaginative in finding ways to link in to the economic strengths of professional activity, finding new markets in full-cost postgraduate and post-experience work. Differentiation from the mass of higher education will be crucial in maintaining the professional image.

In the mass market, there is an immense range of activity to be considered. Though a full typology will not be attempted, some possible niches may be worth identifying. At this level, given the likely funding, there will be great difficulty in finding resources to develop good quality courses. Already it seems evident that UK institutions spend too little on educational course development as compared with, say, US institutions. There is a market opportunity for a group of institutions seriously to address the challenge of providing education as a commodity, for sale in packaged form to other institutions and taking full heed of the demanding specification required for modularisation. Local delivery of educational packages prepared and maintained elsewhere is therefore likely to become an increasing feature of the scene, accompanied by strengthening of the external quality controls.

All this suggests that there will be a stratification within the mass-market level into those institutions which create, innovate and update; and those which merely repeat or replicate and are judged on delivery of the courses and support for students. That this requires different kinds of academic staff is obvious: it may become equally obvious that attracting staff of the right kind to the former group of institutions will require that they have research opportunities. It should not be presumed that institutions whose main concern is provision of non-élite higher education are to be excluded from the research league.

One feature of the future scene will be that not all the present institutions are represented in it. There has been great reluctance on the part of government to challenge the need for particular institutions, with occasional intervention occurring only after financial mismanagement. The forces about to be unleashed will not be so kind.

Appendix A: UGC and UFC Funding Systems for Higher Education

In what follows, the discussion is deliberately restricted to England, not because the other parts of the UK are essentially different but because they come under different Funding Councils, so that the details of funding systems are not identical.

Funding Models

In the days of the old University Grants Committee (UGC), it is doubtful whether the term 'funding model' could properly be applied to its method of working. The concept was of a unit of resource per student, depending on subject and level. Each unit of resource – to which was added a separate tuition fee paid in effect directly by government through the mandatory award system administered by the Local Education Authorities – was nominally the same for all universities, though in practice there were many special additions for particular circumstances. There was no overt separation of teaching and research within this unit, so that institutions which spent little on research could afford to spend (or waste) money on teaching to small groups.

Under the UGC, redistribution of funding between institutions depended largely on judgements, reached either at officer level or on advice from subject panels, and was normally expressed by saying that funded student numbers in some specified subject area at the institution were to be increased or decreased. Occasionally, the intervention by the UGC would take the form that funding of a particular subject at the institution was to cease altogether, so that in effect a department would be forced to close, amalgamate with another or – by arrangement, with the UGC as mediator – transfer to another institution.

Essentially, this system did not have the mechanistic features characteristic of a funding model. What it did have, though, was the capability of responding to perceived national needs for graduate numbers in particular subject areas (with all that implies about the difficulties and dangers of 'manpower planning' as the term then was); it also had the capability of addressing quality at the departmental level, though it has to be said that its methodologies were far from transparent and by no means accepted as fair by all institutions. However, it lacked detailed powers to intervene at the still-finer subdivision of particular courses: universities were thus able to mount such courses as they thought fit.

By contrast, the central funding and regulatory mechanisms in the former polytechnic sector were more interventionist still: course approval was necessary, not only through the CNAA in terms of educational quality and standards but also through the Department of Education mechanisms which attempted to ensure that local provision of courses avoided unnecessary duplication (in conformity with the anti-competitive policies of the time). Unit of resource calculations in higher education within the sector were complicated by the co-existence of further and higher education, in principle separately funded, but without effective ring-fencing.

Events were to show that the resource per student in higher education was to fall dramatically in both sectors. The polytechnic sector began the 1970s with a unit of teaching resource – for its very few such students – which was actually higher than the corresponding unit for the universities. The decade saw a considerable shift, with the polytechnics taking the bulk of the growth in student numbers and beginning the 1980s with a unit of resource substantially below that of the universities. This was the period of maximum tension and jealousy between the two sectors, compounded by the 1981 cuts in resource flowing to the universities and by the growing resentment that the top universities were protected from ill-effects by their fat cushion of research funding.

The White Paper on Higher Education (HMSO, 1987) foresaw a large increase in the age-participation rate, rising from 20 per cent to 33 per cent of the age cohort entering higher education by the end of the century, though it was silent as to the way in which this huge expansion was to be financed. This heralded the era of the Universities Funding Council, which strongly encouraged expansion by means of a funding model intended to penalise those institutions which fell below expansion targets and reward those which over-recruited.

The Instability of the UFC Funding Model of 1991

It was readily possible to show that this funding model was inherently unstable, and that its application as planned would lead to collapse of the system (within three to five years) through bankruptcy of some institutions and calamitous overstretching of the physical resources of others. The effects of the excessive momentum generated by this ill-advised model for teaching funding are still being felt.[1]

In 1991, the Universities Funding Council announced funding numbers for 1991/92 only but indicated that further funding numbers would depend on the performance of institutions in recruiting students, with clawback of grant if numbers fell below target and with re-allocation of extra funded numbers being governed by the extent to which numbers were above target. Although this was to be done according to discrete subject pools, not on an institutional basis, it was of interest to project the effects of this process as if it applied uniformly across an institution.

Assumptions of the Projection

It was assumed in the projection that the UFC unit of teaching resource per funded home/EC student remained constant and, for illustrative purposes, that the tuition fee represented half the unit of resource. (For arts subjects, the actual fee was about two-thirds of the unit of resource and for science subjects, about one-third). It was further assumed that, as announced, the UFC would increase funded numbers overall at 2·8 per cent per annum. However, an expansion in total numbers of just over 5 per cent per annum was expected for the university system, based on fees-only students. These figures were consistent with the (then) Department of Education and Science's Autumn statement, which gave the projected actual size of the UFC sector as 343,000 fte for 1991/92 and 363,000 for 1992/93.

Methodology

Five institutions A-E were modelled (as if together they

---

[1] This section is based on a memorandum written by R.N. Franklin and A.H. Seville, circulated privately to the CVCP and to the Funding Councils, which served at the time to heighten awareness of the importance of these matters in the determination of funding policy.

represented the whole system), each with different assumptions about growth rate of total student numbers, being +15 per cent, 10 per cent, 5 per cent, 0 per cent and -5 per cent respectively. These student numbers were then compared with the target numbers which determined re-allocation or clawback.

Three projections were made for these target numbers:

Projection X used UFC funded numbers as the target numbers for both re-allocation and clawback. The clawback was simply the amount by which the actual numbers in the previous year fell below the funded numbers in that year. Extra funded numbers were then given to other institutions in proportion to their excess of actual numbers over the funded numbers, again in the previous year.

Projection Y used the system average numbers as targets for both clawback and re-allocation.

Projection Z combined both approaches, using funded numbers as clawback targets and system average numbers as re-allocation targets.

For each projection, a set of three curves was calculated showing respectively:

- UFC funded numbers, shown as 1·00 as the starting value in each case, but recalculated from year to year.

- Total student numbers, calculated on the growth rate assumptions.

- Unit of resource, obtained by dividing total funding by total student numbers.

Only the curves for projection Z are reproduced here (Figures 3-5, pp. 113-15).

Discussion of the Projections

Projection X was relatively benign. Institution A doubled in size, increased funded numbers by 47 per cent, and found itself with an average unit of resource of 0·78. Institution D remained static. Institution E shrunk, with little compensation in terms of unit of resource.

Projection Y was catastrophic and had to be terminated at year 4. Even so, Institution E had by then lost three-quarters of its funded numbers. Even Institution D lost almost half of its UFC funding, though maintaining a steady state 5 per cent above its original funded numbers. In fact, the transfer of funded numbers was so rapid that even A could not keep up. The model was not realistic, but showed what could happen if the Funding Council had attempted to claw back from institutions which were meeting funded number targets but were keeping below the system average numbers – a possibility mentioned by the UFC at the time.

Projection Z appears to be the most realistic of the three. Institutions A and B benefited by comparison with projection X, at the expense of institution C, which gains little in resource unit terms from its restraint on growth. Institution D was, on the other hand, not penalised for its failure to grow.

These projections showed how seriously the university system can be affected by what may appear slight changes in the resource allocation mechanism and how institutions individually can suffer or benefit in ways which are essentially arbitrary as a result.

Although the model has been superseded, it is of some current interest since it moved the system quite close to one of fully-transferable student-based resource, where funding of an institution would depend only on the number of full-time-equivalent students enrolled in any year, and their subject category – that is, a system without any 'historic' funding and without restrictions on numbers other than those imposed by the institutions themselves. This would, for example, be the case if a 'voucher' system were implemented.

More positively, though, the UFC completed the task, begun in the latter years of the UGC, of separating the funding of research from the funding of teaching, developing a model for the selective allocation of research funds on the basis of volume and quality measures.

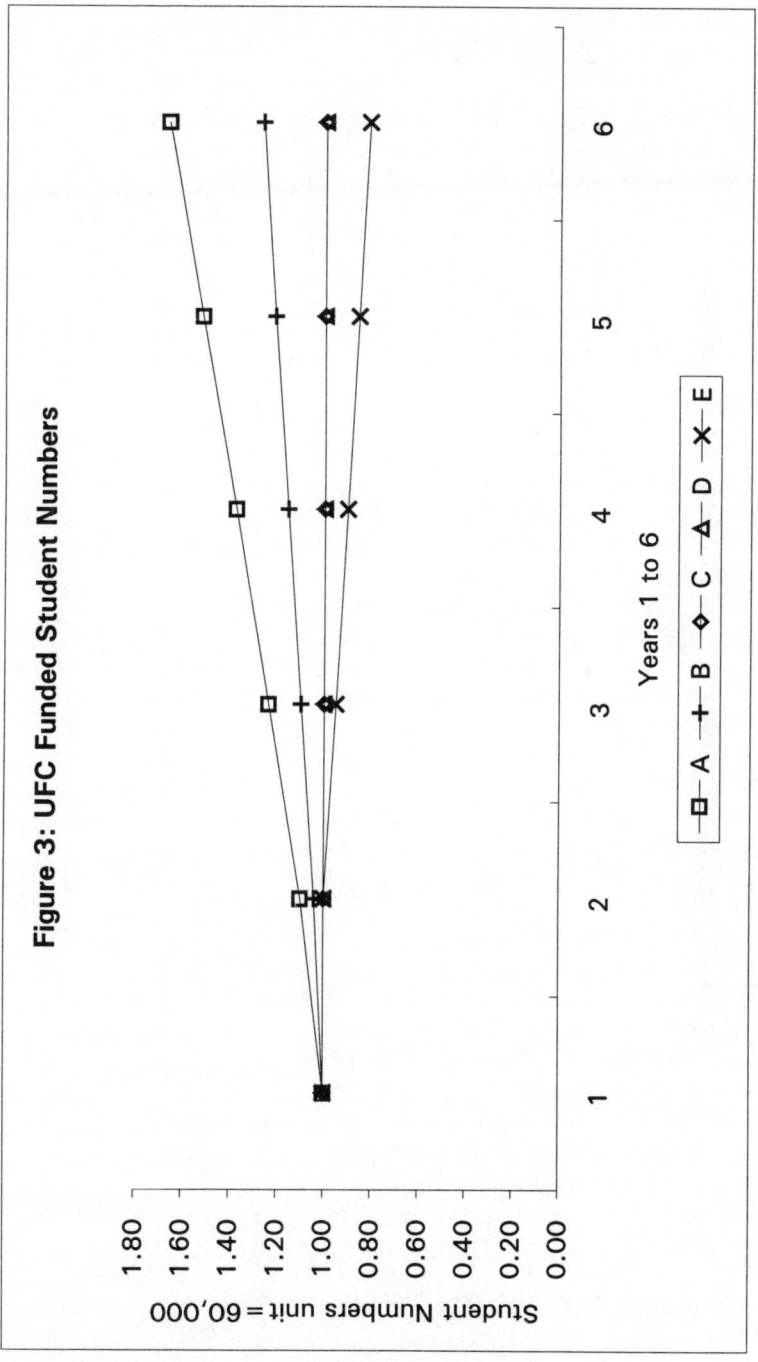

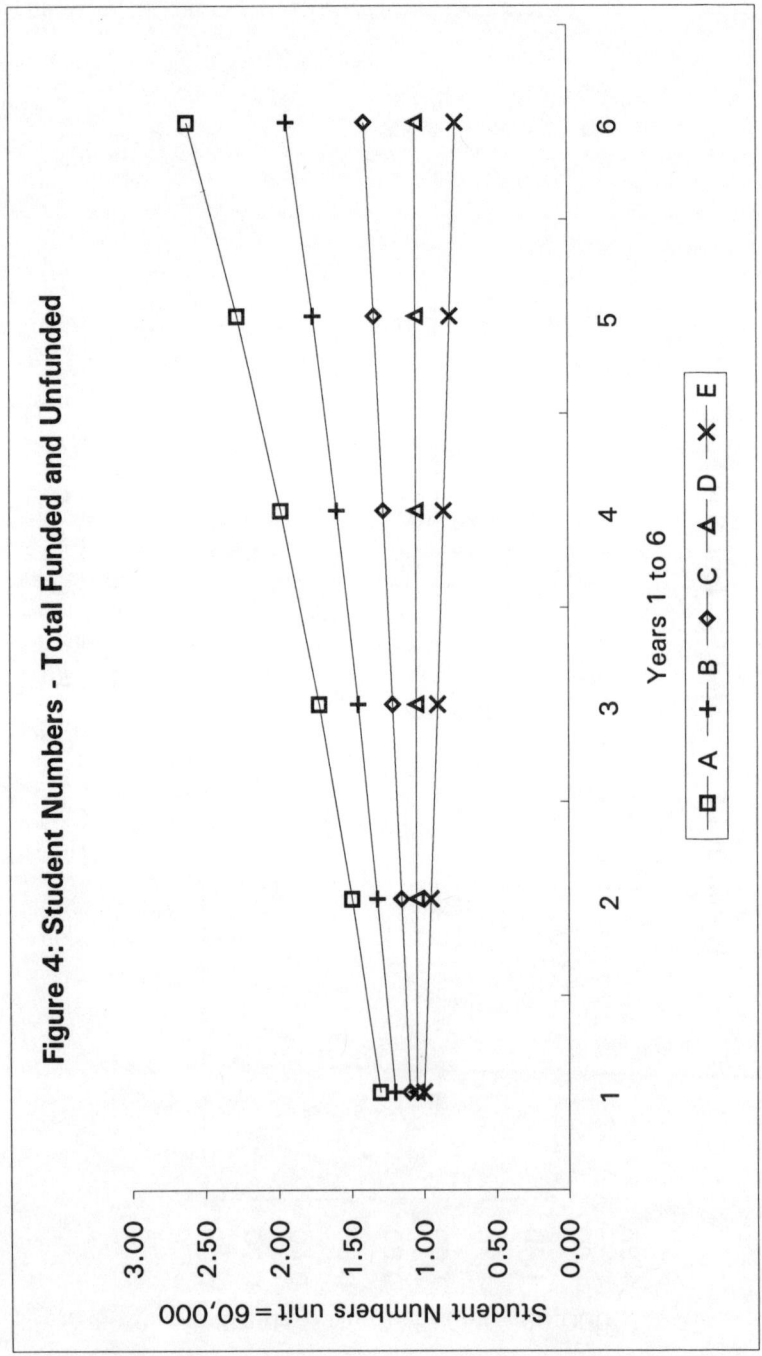

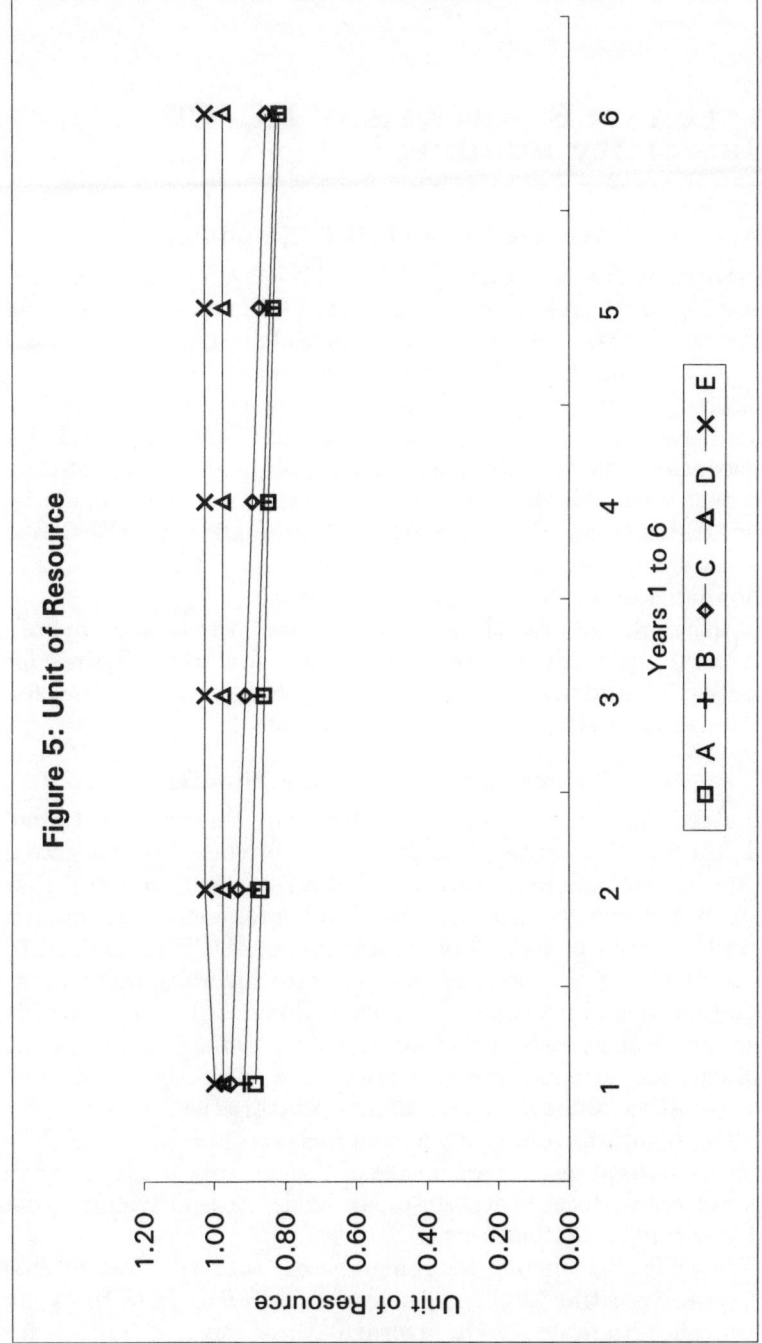

Appendix B: Analysis of HEFCE University Funding

Average Units of HEFCE Funding

Average units of council funding (AUCF) for the academic year 1993-94 are given in the HEFCE report no. 1/94 of August 1994. The report tabulates the AUCF and corresponding home/EU student numbers for each funded institution for each of 10 academic subject categories (ASC). Separate figures are given for taught students and for research students, with a separation of full-time and part-time in each case. All these figures are based on returns made by the institutions which are invited annually by HEFCE to break down their grant total to indicate how it is spent within the institution.

Although the breakdown is not audited, the figures for full-time taught students are not seriously distorted; figures for part-time students are likely to mislead because of inconsistent conversion to full-time-equivalent.

Comparison of Teaching Funding

The comparison of teaching funding was therefore restricted to full-time students. It is then easy to compare the actual funding for teaching received by an institution with that which it would receive if it were funded for each student on a strict formula basis at the system-mean AUCF in each ASC. A comparison was done for all general university institutions (excluding non-university and specialist institutions) outside London and excluding Oxford and Cambridge because of the college fee arrangements. This gave a group of 30 'old' universities and a group of 28 'new' universities.

The resultant comparisons, in which actual HEFCE funding was expressed as a percentage of the formula funding which would result from a system-mean basis, ranged widely, from 58 per cent to 121 per cent.

However, it should be remembered that the institutions also received the 1993/94 standard tuition fees from the state for undergraduates. On average, these fees accounted for about 56 per cent of the total teaching funding received for undergraduates by institutions. They also received postgraduate tuition fees of at least the standard rate. Adding in these standard fees reduced the actual funding range for institutions considerably, the range being 89 per cent to 109 per cent. A regression of actual funding against the system-mean formula shows that about 98 per cent of the actual funding would have been reproduced on the formula basis. The bar graph (Figure 6) summarises the results obtained, plotting the number of institutions falling in each percentage funding range.

The comparison between old and new universities is interesting, the percentage means for the two groups being 100·8 and 98·3 respectively. If the three new institutions at the skewed bottom end are excluded, the corresponding mean for the group becomes 99·8, which is not significantly different from that of the other group.

For subsequent years, the proportion of funding attributable to fee income has been reduced, with limited compensation given on a formula basis in the HEFCE grant. These changes prevent any direct comparison year-on-year, which would otherwise be expected to show a convergence of funding towards the system-mean basis, because of the operation of the HEFCE funding model.

The conclusion is that the system, apart from a few outlying institutions, is quite close to formula funding. It should be remembered that institutions are not able to predict actual student numbers with exactness, so that discrepancies of funding within one or two per cent are natural to the system.

It is of interest that the HEFCE in its 1996 consultation on teaching funding is proposing to move to a uniform allocation model, based on the system mean but allowing for discrepancies of plus or minus 5 per cent in the institutional overall AUCF, to permit some flexibility of under- and over-recruitment.

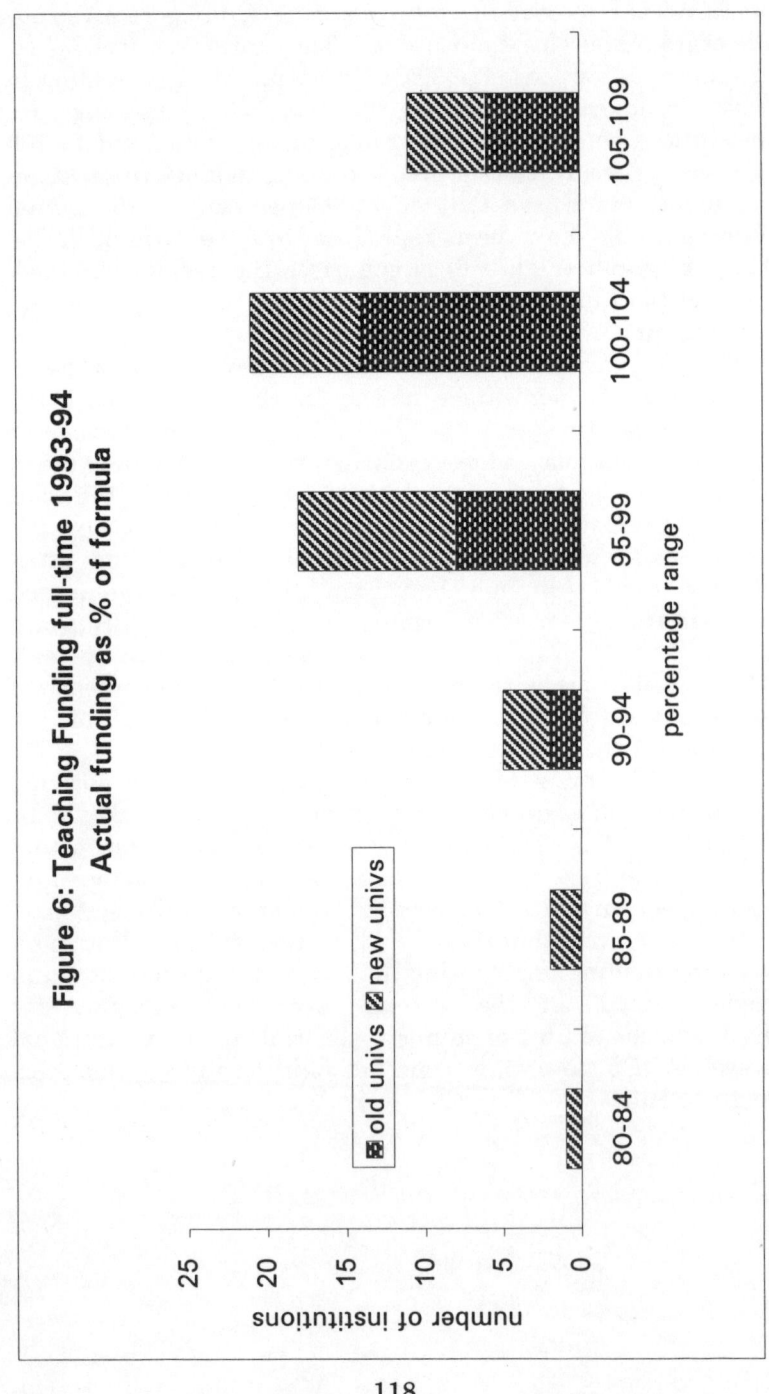

References/Bibliography

Committee of Vice-Chancellors and Principals (1994): *University Management Statistics and Performance Indicators in the UK*, CVCP.

Connor, H., Pearson, R., Court, G., and Jagger, N. (1996): *University Challenge – Student Choices in the 21st Century*, Brighton: University of Sussex, Institute for Employment Studies (Report 306).

Department for Education and Employment (1996): *DfEE/HE Sector Working Party on The Effects of Public Funding on HE Institutions*, DfEE.

Employment Department (1995): *A Vision for Higher Level Vocational Qualifications – Competence and Assessment*, No. 29, pp. 2-4.

Franklin, R. N., and Seville, A. H. (1992): (private communication).

Higher Education Funding Council for England (1993): *Report of the Committee on Organisation of the Academic Year*, Bristol: HEFCE.

Higher Education Funding Council for England (1996): *Funding Method for Teaching*, Consultation 1/96, Bristol: HEFCE.

Higher Education Quality Council (1994): *Choosing to Change: the report of the HEQC CAT Development Project*, London: HEQC.

Higher Education Quality Council (1995): *Choosing to Change: Outcomes of the Consultation*, London: HEQC.

Higher Education Quality Council (1996): *What is a Graduate?*, London: HEQC.

HESA (1995): *Education Statistics for the United Kingdom 1992/93*, Higher Education Statistics Agency.

HMSO (1987): *Higher Education – Meeting the Challenge*, London: Her Majesty's Stationery Office.

Silver, H., Stennett, A., and Williams, R. (1995): *The External Examiner System: Possible Futures*, London: Higher Education Quality Council/Quality Support Centre.

Watson, D. (1989): *Managing the Modular Course*, Oxford: Society for Research in Higher Education/Oxford University Press.

Williams, G., and Fry, H. (1994): *Longer Term Prospects for Higher Education*, Centre for Higher Education Studies, Institute of Education, University of London.